Amid the Swirling Ghosts
and
Other Essays

Amid the Swirling Ghosts and Other Essays

William Caverlee

University of Louisiana at Lafayette Press
2009

University of Louisiana at Lafayette Press
P.O. Box 40831
Lafayette, LA 70504-0831
http://cls.louisiana.edu

ISBN 13 (paper): 978-1-887366-92-2
ISBN 10 (paper): 1-887366-92-X

Library of Congress Cataloging-in-Publication Data

Caverlee, William.
Amid the swirling ghosts, and other essays / William Caverlee.
p. cm.
ISBN-13: 978-1-887366-92-2 (pbk. : alk. paper)
ISBN-10: 1-887366-92-X (pbk. : alk. paper)
1. American literature--Southern States--History and criticism. I. Title.
PS261.C38 2009
810.9'975--dc22

2009027916

Printed on acid-free paper.

Front cover illustration: "Poet's House" (1999) by Maggie Taylor; used by permission.

Contents

Acknowledgments

Grateful thanks to the editors of *The Oxford American Magazine* and *The Christian Science Monitor*, where many of the essays here were first published, some in a slightly different form. A bibliography, a list of original publications, and a note on sources are found at the back of the book.

Special thanks also to Michael Breed, Charles deGravelles, and Lea Olsan Jones—friends, fellow writers, and the best of teachers.

Foreword

When William Caverlee's essay on William Faulkner's *The Sound and the Fury* snuck into our office as a "blind" (i.e., unassigned, unexpected, unasked-for) submission none of us at *The Oxford American* had heard of him—Caverlee, I mean. On top of that, no editor here felt a special urge to publish an essay extolling the virtues of Faulkner's dog-eared masterpiece. Who needed a critic to point out that *The Sound and the Fury* is one of the signal achievements of Southern literature?

By the end of Caverlee's submission (the title piece of this collection), I had changed my tune. Caverlee's sprightly approach to this "improbable novel" and his lucid, playful insight into Faulkner's "ridiculous syntax . . . obsessions, oddities . . . [and] lofty talk of honor, family, the past" suddenly made Faulkner a little more understandable or understandable in a fresh way—no mean feat. (I am not alone in my praise; a number of *Oxford American* readers told me that Caverlee inspired them to revisit Faulkner's novel.)

The Caverlee lesson is that there is always a need for insightful, probing, and eloquent criticism—even when talking about familiar and older works. Just as *The Sound and the Fury* is one of the most discussed novels of Southern literature, Flannery O'Connor's 1953 "A Good Man Is Hard to Find" is one of its most discussed stories. So, of course, Caverlee takes on "A Good Man Is Hard to Find" in another essay in this book. And what does he do? The same thing he did with the Faulkner book—he writes with so much verve and intelligence that he will likely prompt readers to rush out to revisit the story.

The mainstream media likes to make it seem that only new "product" has value or meaning. But if an old work retains merit, real-life people—like you or me—will still engage old books, old stories, old movies, and old music. This suggests that many of us don't buy into mainstream media efforts to make us only consider—and purchase—the New. Quality remains more important than vintage. In treating the good old stuff with respect and perspicacity, Caverlee the critic provides a subtle if not radical service. He's challenging the status quo—inadvertently or not, he's a one-man crusade standing up to the Big Red and Blue Machine of mainstream media and mainstream marketing. Let 'er rip, Bill!

Finally, I would like to point out that superficial and shrill criticism, of which there is too much, can make a lot of people think that all criticism is petulant, petty, and facile nay-saying. But that's *bad* criticism. Let's separate bad criticism from good criticism. Good criticism brings value to our households in various ways. For example, good criticism can introduce us to art—books, stories, movies, albums, etc.—that we wouldn't have found otherwise, on our own. (There are many examples in my own life when a critic led me to a new love.) And when it comes to art that we think we already know, good criticism can deepen our perception of the familiar, and thus our enjoyment.

Caverlee does more in this collection than criticize. He is a writer of vast enthusiasms and range. The essay, when well done, just happens to be one of my favorite forms. I've also learned there's something oddly enduring about penetrating and well-written literary criticism: it can last as long as the literature it examines, and it can even take on the name of literature itself.

Read on and see for yourself.

Marc Smirnoff, editor
The Oxford American

1

DESPERADOES, HEROES, MOVIES

Bullets and Bodies

About an hour's drive from the room where I am writing is the Bonnie and Clyde ambush site—a small rise on Louisiana Highway 154, off Interstate 20, between Gibsland and Sailes. In 1934, as every moviegoer knows, a squad of six earnest and determined lawmen fired a hundred and thirty rounds into the two outlaws, killing them in the front seat of their Ford V-8—not separately as in the movie version, with Warren Beatty standing outside the car eating a pear, but together, in the front seat, in cold blood (no Miranda rights in 1934). The two Texans were due for a killing, being thugs and murderers on the Dillinger scale. Bonnie had even predicted such an outcome in her poetry.

The anonymous country road is still there, as is the nearby town, Arcadia, where the riddled Ford and the two bodies were towed. One legend has it that when the lawmen towed the Ford past a little country school in Gibsland, a crowd of schoolchildren poured into the road to get a better look. They pressed excitedly up against the car—the two slumped bodies still inside—and for a second it seemed that they might push themselves right into the front seat; that is, until they were close enough to see the blood and the shattered faces, and then they started vomiting. When the Ford reached Arcadia, thousands of townspeople and farm folk swarmed into the streets, pushing right into Conger's Furniture Store and Funeral Parlor, the cops trying to keep order, souvenir hunters scrounging about, everyone impatient for the coroner to finish his work and display the bodies. That display was preserved for us, too, in photographs and a black-and-white newsreel (a copy of which I'd found at the parish library), artifacts which add yet another layer to the referential craziness Bonnie and Clyde evoke. Bonnie was twenty-three years old when they killed her; Clyde was twenty-five.

For the two Texans, north Louisiana was a place of refuge after fundraising jaunts through Missouri, Kansas, and Oklahoma. In the 1930s, the rural parishes and villages of the region were as distant from Bonnie and Clyde's home base in Dallas as was South America—the Louisiana pine forests making an impenetrable and useful hideout.

Here, in north Louisiana, we are only three or four generations away from our literature's ever-pressing stream of Scotch-Irish farmers, gamblers, and dreamers who leap-frogged from the Carolinas into Alabama, Mississippi, and Louisiana. Carrying our Bibles, guns, plows, intransigence. Every conceivable form of Protestantism and self-invented sect besides. Deer hunters, hard-pan farmers, Snopes after Snopes after Snopes, with an easy fluency in guns, death, meat-butchering, loss, and sin—a lethal, believing/unbelieving white man's nation from the Mississippi River to the Texas line.

Clyde Barrow was the genetic culmination of a long line of east Texas farm types, practicing and fulfilling every cliché of his ilk: theft, assault, jail breaks, vendettas, and violent death. He was a sawed-off little sociopath, a ten-time loser, and his gang's twelve murder victims have had no movies made about them, no symposia hosted by cinéastes, no articulation by the French New Wave.

Few of us still visit the death site on Highway 154. What's the point? We know what a two-lane blacktop road in Bienville Parish looks like. We know where red-tailed hawks like to perch along fields and roadways; what a spring day in May feels like, with the astounding heat and a haze of gnats in the air. On a particularly oppressive morning like the one in 1934, with the law hiding in trees and bushes, the heat is said to be *close*. Still, another kind of spring surrounded the ambushers had they cared to look: the annual eruption of ten thousand flowers and plants—azaleas, wisteria, wild plum, dogwood, jonquils, forsythia, quince. Blooming one after the other, or sometimes all at once, each improbable color overlaid upon another, dizzying to behold, in both woodland and town. In director Arthur Penn's film, in this last scene, blood is the most vivid color—but could the woods instead have been in full bloom, we wonder, as the six hidden men took careful aim?

It's strange to realize that more years have passed since the release of the film *Bonnie and Clyde* than passed between the actual events and their appropriation by Hollywood in 1967. Around here, predictably, the movie was as notorious for Faye Dunaway's partial nudity in the opening scene as her death spasms at the film's close. Flesh exposed, flesh perforated—take your pick. And everything coming to an end with all those torrents of bright red blood, offered to us in the voluptuousness of Technicolor film.

In 1967, those of us who saw *Bonnie and Clyde* in the small towns of north Louisiana walked out of the theaters in a kind of daze—moved, shocked, silent, and perhaps secretly exhilarated. But we had no clue about the film's French origins, of Beatty's and Arthur Penn's complex, high-art vision (traced deftly by Louis Menand in a *New Yorker* article in 2003). By now, the making of the film is freighted with nearly as much mythology and speculation as its subject: The screenwriters, David Newman and Robert Benton, composing their gangster-treatment with inspiration from French film; the early negotiations with French director François Truffaut; Beatty's purchase of the script—Truffaut out, Arthur Penn in, then screenwriter Robert Towne entering the fray. All these legends becoming an endless meal for critics, film historians, and students. Truffaut, of course, wrote the original screenplay for *Breathless* (1959), filmed by Jean-Luc Godard, with Jean-Paul Belmondo as a two-bit outlaw on the run from the French cops with his American girlfriend, famously and laconically portrayed by Jean Seberg. All that plus a bloody shootout at film's end. Cinema buffs love to speak of the New Wave's excitement upon encountering American slang, gangsters, car chases, blondes. Thus *Bonnie and Clyde* as an American response to the French response to American film.

Or, as some would have it, as a response to the Kennedy assassination—a conjecture that is no great stretch for the amateur film critic.

In the old black-and-white World War II movies, when an American soldier was killed, he died bloodlessly from a quick bullet. A brief groan, then instantly dead. Or better still, a nonfatal shoulder wound that could be repaired with a handy bandage, a short spell in the infirmary, some all-American joshing with a wisecracking nurse named Alice or Josie, then back to the front lines, fit as a fiddle.

The wartime censorship of news photos and film was voluntary and, for the most part, unquestioned. Everyone apparently was in agreement that the mothers and fathers of the American home front would collapse, their morale shattered, if they viewed the destroyed bodies of their children. Hollywood complied. After the war, millions of G.I.s tended to keep their war experiences guarded. That silence was later bequeathed to the rest of us in terms of the stereotypical '50s American father—detached and emotionally unavailable. Wives, parents, children, the whole country seemed to say: "Well, O.K., if you don't want to talk about it, that's fine with us." And, as a substitute national therapy, we were given John Wayne.

Kennedy's death put an end to all that—specifically, the third bullet, the death shot to the head. The president's assassination was cataclysmic in itself, whether you heard about it by radio, television, or newspaper. But it was that final hideous bullet, inadvertently captured on Zapruder's film, that revealed forever, and on every newspaper in the land, what an entire generation had suppressed since World War II—the effect of a high-powered rifle shot on human tissue and bone. (The horror even greater a few years later when we could watch the full sequence over and over on film and television.) Was Penn influenced by any of this? Yes. In a 1967 interview in *Cahiers du Cinéma*, he refers to "a piece of Warren's head which flies off like Kennedy's in the famous photo of his death." Whatever the case, for the rest of us, when we watch the convulsing bodies in *Bonnie and Clyde*, it's not hard to track the unprecedented shock effect of 1967 back to the Zapruder film—its anatomical clarity, its terrible pink mist.

Meanwhile, Highway 154 endures. The pine woods of north Louisiana have been clearcut, regrown, and cut again. When I visited the ambush site late last year, the forest lay on all sides and the sense of deep hiddenness had hardly changed—with the ghosts of the real Parker and Barrow no doubt lurking about somewhere, youngsters who in 1934 were themselves as media-savvy as their future hagiographers, Beatty and Penn. Offering the national newspapers a running commentary on their own notoriety—Bonnie's famous cigar-smoking photograph (holding a revolver, her foot on a Ford's front bumper), her poetry to the public, antics with lawmen, a purported letter to Henry Ford, praising his autos.

Rumor has it that some of the bullets passed straight through the driver-side door, through Clyde's body, then through Bonnie, then through the opposite door, before exiting the Ford and landing in some pine tree or dirt embankment, to be dug up later that day by a Bienville Parish souvenir hunter, whose descendant, seventy years later, would comb the same woods with a metal detector and a GPS. A hundred and thirty rounds. Or two hundred? The various accounts—the various mythologies—are not clear on this point. The same uncertainty holds for the number of Bonnie and Clyde's murder victims. Twelve? Thirteen? Fourteen? And did Bonnie kill anyone? No, never, yes, and maybe. There's a book, an author, a school, for any position you may wish to take. Then there's the couple's sexual hijinks. Did they engage in threesomes with other gang members? Were they a pair of romantic Depression Age underdogs, or just two more blank-faced, half-literate murderers—grocery-store and gas-station bandits—barely competent in their chosen field?

A nagging question, some detail or other that I need to check on, takes me back to that silent newsreel at the parish library, and after a minute or two of searching, I find it. And later, watching at home, yes, here are Barrow and Parker; here's footage of the ambush site, then the death car; then two bodies on the mortuary slab; and then, holding still for several seconds, the camera records Bonnie's naked breast, unmarked, intact—a scene of necrophilial American voyeurism. *Pure cinema* . . . And then, for a moment, in one of those grotesque dreamy convergences I'd rather not think about outside a shrink's office, the vision of dead, naked Bonnie merges with the Zapruder nightmare and be-spattered Faye Dunaway and a thousand other TV and movie corpses and shoot-out scenes, as well as all those pictures of Playmates and starlets I sought out and pored over through the 1960s and '70s, all the way up to the 1975 photo-spread of Jackie O, naked in *Hustler*, full-frontal on a Greek island in some paparazzo's telephoto shot, the voyeuristic circle now complete by none other than the former First Lady herself, after which a kind of finality and sadness settled over America.

The cities of Monroe, Ruston, and Shreveport link up east-to-west along Interstate 20, in a hundred-mile band of American modernity, with the usual restaurant names, malls, billboards, and frontage roads. You have to press deeper into the woods to resuscitate the 1930s.

So you drive further, no longer stopping at the named towns—Arcadia, Homer, Eros, Athens—until you reach a mere crossroads. And, yes, here is an actual old-time tent revival in progress, with shouts and clamors, joyful bodies flopping on the ground, salvation and ecstasy found in canvas tents. It is sometimes only a matter of turning left or turning right that destines a child to a lifetime of preaching or of predation. Or maybe both, if you're someone like Flannery O'Connor's The Misfit. There are a dozen pickup trucks parked in a muddy field and a fastness of pine trees just past the clearing, beyond which there is no sound at all, only deep woods.

The old Southern novelists expended millions of words tracing out the emanations from those deep woods, following the paths of their Popeyes and Misfits, from the forests to the towns and back again. Out-done only by nonfiction, by the newborn Hazel Moteses and Bonnies and Clydes that the South never seems to run out of. Faulkner, O'Connor, Welty, Percy—it's not hard to see how they became addicted to it all, the voluptuousness of God, sex, and violence.

Around 1967, at age seventeen, I tagged along once with my older brother on an errand to the bank. (Not far away, *Bonnie and Clyde* was playing at a downtown theater.) In the lobby, we bumped into the bank president, who paused for a quick chat. He was a breezy rural millionaire, straight out of the logging roads and oil fields, an old-style Earl Long, lapel-grabbing, shoulder-squeezing Louisiana pol. After a few jokes, he glanced down at me, then remarked: "This one's going to be fine one day, he just needs to get himself a little *mean*." Such wisdom would have been easily comprehended by Clyde Barrow's father, or by Earl and Huey Long's father.

In the spring of 1934, the families of Barrow and Parker came to Louisiana and took the two bodies back to Texas and gave them good Christian burials, with flowers, tombstones, and throngs of mourners. Some later wrote books, others gave interviews, one or two went on the lecture circuit.

On location—a pleasant-enough country road with plenty of trees and sunshine but no spring flowers, no blooms at all—Warren Beatty pretends to hear a sudden rush of birds lifting from the trees and then exchanges a last panicked look with Faye Dunaway in the front seat of her Hollywood Ford V-8.

The Unenthusiastic Chess Champion of the World

Three hundred years of history and [New Orleans] has never produced a single significant historical event, one single genius, or even a first-class talent—except a chess player, the world's greatest.

– Walker Percy

The first Paul Morphy legend is born in 1846. General Winfield Scott, on his way to the U.S.-Mexican War, stops off in New Orleans and makes inquiries about setting up a chess game with a local. Certain New Orleanians (roguishly? sardonically?) answer that they know just the person. That night, in a chess club on Royal Street, General Scott is introduced to an eight-and-a-half-year-old boy. Scott nearly walks out in indignation, but then agrees to play. The boy checkmates the general in ten moves.

As a grown man, Morphy was five feet, four inches tall. Slender, delicate. Aristocratic touches came honestly: His father was a Louisiana Supreme Court justice; his family belonged to New Orleans' social elite, with addresses on Chartres Street, Royal Street, and at the Pontalba building. On first meeting him, competitors and onlookers sometimes mistook him for a young boy—he was so tiny, with those strange Southern manners, that meekness and eerie quietness. Over four weeks in 1857, Morphy won every match he played at a national chess championship in New York. Two years later, after a similar rout of European players, the chess clubs of London (as well as the American clubs, the press, and every pundit and orator of the day) dubbed him the "Chess Champion of the World."

Today, the name Paul Morphy is nearly forgotten—except by chess enthusiasts. In *their* world, he's still revered, studied, and romanticized—the Napoleon of chess, a comet appearing suddenly in the sky. For chess players, Morphy is the nineteenth-century forerunner of Bobby Fischer—their names are routinely linked in magazine articles, books, and online disputations—two American celebrities, each of them prodigies, each with intensely troubled post-chess lives. Fischer himself once said of his predecessor: "A popularly held theory about Paul Morphy is that if he returned to the chess world today and played our best contemporary players, he would come out the loser. Nothing is further from the truth. In a set match, Morphy would beat anybody alive today."

In 1857, Morphy was untested outside New Orleans when he set off for the tournament in New York, a convocation billed as the First National Chess Congress. He traveled by steamboat up the Mississippi and the Ohio to Cincinnati, then by train to New York, a journey of eleven days. He almost didn't make the trip, even though for months the New York promoters had listed him on publicity sheets and news releases—the Creole genius, the wunderkind from the Gulf of Mexico (they sound like golf-tournament sponsors banking on a Tiger Woods appearance). But he had family complications. His father had died the previous year—the result of an absurd accident—turning in a crowd and cutting his eye on someone's Panama hat, followed by infection, two months in bed, decline and death. Familiar themes of life in nineteenth-century New Orleans—family, grief, oddity, death.

There are numerous likenesses of Morphy from the era—a photograph by Matthew Brady; a drawing by Winslow Homer; oil paintings by Elliott, Carvalho, and Rosenbaum; a marble bust by the French sculptor Eugene Lequesne . . . newspaper engravings, daguerreotypes, tintypes. Morphy is always in a formal white shirt, collar, tie, waistcoat, and a long dark frock coat—standing in a photographer's studio with his arm on a chair or on a draped table or some kind of faux-pedestal, its top surface about elbow-height, with carved wooden moldings, just the right touch for a hint of the classical.

And he looks small even in the photographs and engravings—eyes downcast, somber; or else wide-open, distant. A strong chin though. These are formal sittings, not snapshots taken on Canal Street. The marble bust by Lequesne (made when Morphy was in France in 1858) has a slight, curious resemblance to T.E. Lawrence. It portrays Morphy looking straight ahead, with high cheekbones, a sensual full lower lip, the upper lip less so, but with a prominent philtrum. A broad clear forehead. And then that haircut! (No Lawrence comparison there.) Lequesne tones down Morphy's nineteenth century pompadour—but you can't help thinking of all those photographs of Civil War generals posing sternly in their uniforms, hat in hand. Their hair always looks stiff and greasy—maybe it's just barbershop tonic.

During his undergraduate days with the Jesuits at Spring Hill College in Mobile, Alabama, Morphy rarely played chess. Instead, he focused on languages, philosophy, mathematics, science, and drama. For the Philomatic Society at Spring Hill, he delivered a lecture on "Astronomy & particularly the discovery of the Planet Le Verrier & those of Sir Wm. Herschel among the Nebula." After Spring Hill, he returned home and earned a law degree at age nineteen from the University of Louisiana. He considered himself primarily a lawyer.

Chess historians have archived hundreds of Morphy's matches, which they annotate, argue over, and replay on websites and coffeehouse boards all over the world. Morphy's 1858 game against two noblemen, the Duke of Brunswick and Count Isouard, has long been considered a classic. Morphy (playing White) checkmated his two opponents in only seventeen moves. (It wasn't unusual for him to play two men at once. There were other stunts: He sometimes played "blindfolded"—against seven or eight opponents simultaneously—and not on seven or eight boards, but solely in his mind, calling out his moves, "Board One, Board Two," etc.)

The Duke and the Count played Morphy in the Duke's box at the Paris Opera—with Morphy's back to the stage. A performance of *The Barber of Seville* went on behind him. Does the Duke have a place in history other than as one of Morphy's victims? Yes, as a footnote: He was a gloriously improbable freak even by the standards of the day—a German-born Parisian roué, a jewel collector, a dispossessed mad millionaire and gourmand who lived in a booby-trapped Gothic palace, wore makeup, dyed his beard, and attended soirées in fantastical costumes with diamonds in his underwear.

The Opera game (as it came to be called) can be divided into four segments.

1. The players make a few preliminary maneuvers.
2. A brief flurry of combat, with pieces lost on both sides.
3. The two sides once again vie for position; more pieces fall; then, everything seems to come to a halt.

4. There's a silence. Both of Morphy's knights have been lost, but his two bishops are aimed in the direction of the Black king. Morphy's queen and rook are also lurking. The noblemen's king hasn't budged the entire game, having been blocked from escape by its own pieces. Then Morphy makes two swift moves: One of his bishops checks the Black king and in return is taken by an enemy

knight. But this is only a sacrifice, a ploy, and Morphy's queen can now glide to the back row to check Black again. Another sacrifice: The same Black knight easily dispatches Morphy's queen.

Finally (move seventeen), Morphy's rook travels the length of the board to a square directly against the king. *Check.* Maybe one of the noblemen reached instinctively to take the enemy rook with the king. But Morphy's second White bishop, which hadn't captured a single piece, or moved or really done anything for what seems hours, suddenly comes into view as unassailable protection for the rook. *Checkmate.* A character that we didn't pay enough attention to turned out to hold the key to everything.

For nearly twenty years after his public career ended, Morphy lived at home in New Orleans with his family (mother and sister for the most part). New Orleans is known to do that—create citizens who can't live anywhere else. He refused to earn money as a professional chess player—was contemptuous of the idea—but his attempts at practicing law fell short. So what did he do? He read the newspaper, attended the opera, went to the barber shop, took a daily promenade on Canal Street—"always neatly attired," his niece said, "and never without his monocle and his small walking stick."

Wading through various accounts of Morphy's life, we sometimes find ourselves immersed *too* deeply in Victorian refinement. Behind the arch, if not pompous, language of the memoirs, reminiscences, speeches, testimonials, and news articles, we long to catch some glimpse of the man. But can we? Morphy himself spoke in solemn, bookish cadences:

> Chess, hitherto viewed by our countrymen in the light of a mere amusement, assumes at last its appropriate place among the sciences which at once adorn and exalt the intellect. We have met this night to hail the dawn of a true appreciation of its manifold claims to regard. And, gentlemen, may we not cherish the hope

> that this, the first great national gathering of the votaries of Caissa, may prove but the forerunner of many yet to come . . . (Lawson)

He wrote a series of newspaper articles on chess, but left no autobiography, no journals, no diary, just a few dozen letters. We know that Morphy was Roman Catholic. His ancestry—Spanish, French, and Irish. His paternal great-grandfather was named Michael Murphy, the spelling recast as Morphy after the Irishman immigrated for unknown reasons to Spain in the 1750s. Even Morphy's best biographer, David Lawson, cannot quite trace a satisfying outline of the man. Lawson's *Paul Morphy: The Pride and Sorrow of Chess* remains the chief text for Morphy devotees (and the primary source for this essay). The book, 424 slow-moving pages, has long been out of print. Its jacket named Lawson the "world's foremost authority" on Morphy, as well as the "greatest collector of Morphiana," and inside, Lawson boasted of his trophies: e.g., "an inlaid mother-of-pearl chessboard," given to Morphy on his twelfth birthday.

In 1883, the year before Morphy died, the German chess champion Wilhelm Steinitz visited New Orleans and said, "Morphy wants to get married. He is perpetually having 'love affairs.' All the people in New Orleans know it and humor him a little. Mind you, he is the most chivalrous soul alive. He is a thorough gentleman." Everyone may have known it, but not even the usually methodical Lawson can offer any corroboration for this notion. And what about the quotation marks around "love affairs"? Was Steinitz suggesting that it was all a joke—the ludicrous flirtations of an aging *flâneur*? Surely, in the well-stocked fleshpots of New Orleans, there were plenty of occasions for a man to experiment in the arts of love. In 1850, prostitution was New Orleans' second largest economy after the port. Was there some dark-haired woman of his dreams? Or a string of broken hearts, a lost cache of Morphy love letters?

Certainly in Paris, countesses and princesses wanted to meet the American champion, to play chess with him, and Morphy was only too happy to oblige. During these matches, he'd sometimes lose his concentration on the game. Frederick Edge, Morphy's secretary in Europe, wisecracked that he would never bet on Morphy when he played against a woman.

Still, we know that he lived with his mother as a bachelor until he was nearly fifty. Lawson writes of Morphy's widowed mother, the judge's wife:

> Paul's mother, Thelcide . . . had acquired some distinction as a musician and composer. An accomplished pianist and harpist, she also had a fine mezzo-soprano voice and often entertained with musicales . . . Toward the end of her better years, Mrs. Morphy started [to compose] a more ambitious work, the score for a five-act opera, *Louise de Lorraine* . . . But Thelcide got no further than the first four acts, her spirit burdened with increasing concern for Paul in his last years.

It would take a Tennessee Williams or a John Kennedy Toole to elaborate such an entwined mother/son relationship, a familiar Southern theme. Certainly the wrong author for such a work would be Frances Parkinson Keyes, who *did* write a Morphy novel, *The Chess Players* (1960), which easily ranks among the world's worst fiction. Morphy is portrayed as a romantic hero ("he tightened his hold on her waist; and having kissed her throat again and again, found that his lips had strayed until his face was buried in the smooth beauty of the cleft whiteness that rose above her bodice") as well as a Confederate spy in Europe during the Civil War.

Those inanities notwithstanding, Morphy actually hobnobbed with such luminaries as Napoleon III, John Van Buren (son of the president), Longfellow, Oliver Wendell Holmes, and possibly Queen Victoria. Back home in America, Morphy made the rounds of fêtes and testimonials given in his honor. Books appeared praising his exploits. Gifts—a Tiffany chess set ("of the purest Gold and Silver"), a custom-made inscribed watch ("set round with brilliants, with another large diamond at its top"), etc. A group of Brooklynites founded the "Morphy Baseball Club" and made him a member. You could buy a Morphy cigar (imported from Havana), as well as a Morphy hat ("A New and Novel Style of STRAW HAT").

Nearly twenty years after his father died, Morphy suspected his brother-in-law of defrauding him of part of his inheritance, and he filed a futile, interminable lawsuit. He obsessed over the lawsuit; talked of nothing else—to friends, strangers, anyone. Paranoid about enemies, he would only eat food prepared by his sister or mother. He played chess only rarely, with an acquaintance or two, like his oldest friend Charles Maurian. He talked to himself while strolling on the veranda. He believed a barber was in league with a certain Mr. Binder, and one day Morphy attacked Binder and challenged him to a duel (Morphy had taken fencing lessons as a youth—shades of author Keyes!). Morphy's family took him to a Catholic-run mental institution, the "Louisiana Retreat," but when Morphy realized what was happening, he calmly cited the law, convinced the nuns not to admit him, and everyone went back to New Orleans.

Lawson uses reports from the day to establish that Morphy suffered from a mental disorder in his later years. Many examples of odd behavior, persecution mania, obsession, and paranoia abound. On the other hand, Morphy had periods of mental stability—the last year or two of his life were relatively calm. (The case doesn't seem even close to Nabokov's chess novel, *The Defense*, with its grandmaster gone irrevocably insane; nor does it resemble the terrible and bizarre waywardness of Bobby Fischer's last years.) Eminent psychiatrists have their say—studies in the *International Journal of Psycho-Analysis* in 1931 and in *Psychoanalysis Journal*, 1956. A series of scenarios come to mind: The former champion once renowned on two continents, now a man in his forties living at home with his mother and sister in self-imposed isolation and idleness; years of melancholia; eccentricities piled upon eccentricities; a very real anxiety about money and station in life; perfect strangers forever asking him questions about a game, a mere diversion that he'd hoped to leave behind once and for all.

Or . . . Consider Morphy as the heroic artist or sporting figure: At age twenty, he quite literally wanted to conquer the world. This is the fully-oxygenated egomania and narcissism of a Lord Byron or the average presidential candidate—in Morphy's case, combined with aristocratic reticence, cerebral hyperactivity, and a crushing introversion. Lawson, admirably, seems to say: I am not going to speculate any further—this is past all my telling. For the rest of us, whatever the diagnosis, the label, given to Morphy's case, we're left mostly with unanswered questions and a sadness.

If there were a steadying force in Morphy's life, could it have been Charles Maurian, his friend since childhood—Horatio to Morphy's Hamlet? Nearly the same age, they grew up together, went to the same grade schools in New Orleans, then were together during college in Mobile. Again and again, Maurian turns up at critical moments. He was the go-between in family disputes, he wrote letters defending Morphy to New York papers when they published gleeful reports of Morphy's mental decline. Maurian himself was a chess player, although with no illusion that he was anywhere near Morphy's level. Still, they played many games over the years; Morphy gave odds—removing one or more of his pieces.

In a letter of 1875, Maurian observed:

> At that time he told me very frankly that he was going to abandon completely everything in the shape of public chess. But he consented to play with me as often as I should like. After this he went to Europe and on his

> return, observing that he played with me only to please me, I ceased to impose this species of penance on him. Our last games were in 1869 in the month of December.

In the same letter, he defended Morphy against widespread accusations of indolence:

> He is engaged upon no particular business, it is true, but he is fond of literature, an enlightened admirer of the fine arts, a great lover of books and he loves study.

Maurian's dogged loyalty to his old friend is touching, but it's easy to imagine Morphy, in his last years, as more or less an eccentric idler. It is Maurian who offers us an epitaph, when he remarked of Morphy and chess:

> Indeed he never was, strange as it will seem, an enthusiast.

New Orleans in July, an Amazonian experience for those of you who have not lived in Louisiana. On the tenth day of that month, in 1884, Morphy took a morning walk and afterward, as was his habit, a bath. His mother found him in the bathtub, dead. He was forty-seven. Lawson, probably quoting the 1884 medical report, calls it a "congestion of the brain brought on by entering the cold water while very warm after his walk."

He is buried in the Morphy family tomb in St. Louis Cemetery No. 1, the oldest cemetery in the city and known to tourists as the final residence of Marie Laveau, the Voodoo Queen—whose name, rather pointedly, has *not* been forgotten in this three-hundred-year-old city.

Ode to a Hoop Star

I was there—January 31, 1970—at LSU the night Pistol Pete Maravich broke Oscar Robertson's NCAA scoring record. Paid attendance was listed at 11,856—in a building rated for 8,000—but no one in Baton Rouge was surprised by *that.* With so many spectators packed in the aisles, the rafters, the stairs, anywhere, the university's old Cow Palace nearly came apart at the seams during the Maravich era.

Along with my older brother and his wife, I attended every home game that season. Our game-day rituals were as well-rehearsed as the dance team's half-time show: 1) Assemble at 4:00 p.m. at my brother and sister-in-law's house off Nicholson Drive. 2) Make brown-bag lunches—ham and cheese sandwiches, apples, chips, Cokes. Locate our cache of crossword puzzles, magazines, and playing cards—the varsity game didn't begin until 7:45 p.m. and we would need diversions to pass the time. 3) Drive the back way through campus, past the Indian Mounds, past the future site of the Maravich Assembly Center, past the old Huey P. Long Fieldhouse and Tiger Stadium and the Student Union, toward Highland Road, and then—a crucial step here—park a quarter mile short of the arena. 4) Walk the rest of the way down Highland in the mild

Baton Rouge winter, joining the procession of students and diehard general-admission fans who also knew the drill, the throng now becoming festive, joyous, noisy, a small Mardi Gras parade, streaming toward the arena in the January twilight, where, if you arrived by five o'clock, you might find a seat. 5) Eat sandwiches, play cards, watch the freshman game with one eye open. Wait. Wait for 7:45, for Pete's arrival. Number twenty-three . . .

His career scoring record still stands: 3,667 points.

Sports writers keep reminding us of this, and of one additional fact, a datum that needs to be repeated, to be shouted from the rooftops: those 3,667 points were achieved during only three varsity years, not the four years available to today's players. (The next five names on the NCAA scoring list all played for four years.)

3,667 points!

Oh, and another thing . . . achieved without the three-point shot.

What would that have been like? we ask drunkenly, angrily, nearly falling off our bar stools. Pete Maravich with the three-point shot? A scoring machine like Pete, who fed on the crowd's delirium, already routinely made shots from three-point range, from NBA range, from near half-court, simply because there were so few open spots available to him. His standard jump shot? Double-teamed and triple-teamed, and falling backwards to the floor with three or four arms pulling at him, assaulting him, shooting left-handed or right-handed, from the corner, from the bench, from his knees—this frail ectomorph, ridiculously skinny, beaten nearly to death his entire career. At the end of a fifty-point game, his eyes glazed, his wet hair falling stringily in his face, he liked to sign off with a Globetrotter hook shot at the buzzer—Pete resigned, exhausted, but still insouciant, heading to the locker room, like one of us leaving work and tossing an empty Coke into a garbage can, except that Pete was not joking, was capping the evening in an act derived of bravado and youth and fifty thousand practice shots. *This is what is possible, folks. This is the level of the game.* Thirty feet. Buzzer. Swish.

The Cow Palace, a.k.a. the John M. Parker Agricultural Coliseum, was LSU's basketball arena during Pete's entire career. Immense, creaky, defunct, embarrassing even for the rodeo riders and 4-H'ers and equestrians for whom it was intended. One week during my freshman year, my dormitory was overrun by a hundred high-school cowboys in town for an equine convention. The university had put them up for the week in our dorm, in a huge spare room lined with bunkbeds. Our guests went slightly mad that week—rolling bowling balls down the hallway at midnight, spraying fire extinguishers, flooding the showers, dropping water balloons from fifth-floor windows—as if to prove that we LSU dorm residents, who, on anyone's scale, were virtuosos of campus hijinks, were, in fact, milquetoasts compared to a troupe of teens-gone-wild from Alexandria, Natchitoches, and Lake Charles.

My senior year, I lived in a fleatrap apartment off Highland Road, a few hundred yards from the Cow Palace—Pete had left LSU for the pros by then. I walked to class past the old arena every morning—well, those mornings that I went to class. Basketball attendance had declined to—what? A hundred and fifty? Zero? The John M. Parker Agricultural Coliseum was a mausoleum to us now. My last visit to the Cow Palace was to sneak into a Chicago concert—not to avoid the price of a ticket but simply as a lark—taking a sack lunch and hiding out in an upstairs office at five o'clock for an eight o'clock concert, just like going to see Pistol Pete.

But back on that night in January in 1970, my brother and sister-in-law and I took our places not a minute too early—before we knew it, every seat was taken. Pete needed thirty-nine points to break Oscar Robertson's ten-year-old record at the University of

Cincinnati. Thirty-nine points for Pete equaled six or seven points for other mortals—everyone knew he would break the record that night. Television cameras were in place; the game began; Pete appeared. I was nineteen-years-old, sitting with my older brother in the happiest place I knew—at the tail end of a desperate American decade, at the unblemished start of a brand-new decade.

Another number to contemplate: 44.2. His career scoring average. Which is still the NCAA record. (Next highest average: 34.6, Austin Carr of Notre Dame.)

He scored over 50 points twenty-eight times! And did so in the antediluvian basketball era of the 1960s and 1970s. He scored 69 points against Alabama; 66 against Tulane; 64 against Kentucky; 61 against Vanderbilt.

Do the old assistant coaches' scoring charts survive, I wonder, in some basement vault at LSU? Is there a deranged statistician or a recovering basketball maniac somewhere, maybe just released from a mental hospital, who could spend a year extracting the three-pointers from all those dusty dots and scratches, and thus translate into modern numbers Pete's true field goals, percentages, career totals? . . . O Lord, keep us sane, lead us not into speculation.

I saw him once on campus, walking out of Allen Hall with books under his arm, joking with one or two beautiful women. The Beatles haircut, the half-smile. Six-foot-five. I looked away, embarrassed, as if I'd seen an actor backstage, at the end of a performance, before he'd had time to change clothes, to rub off the makeup. I didn't want to see *him*, Pistol Pete, walking through the quad like an ordinary student, like me.

And the team? LSU's basketball team? Of course, we wanted to win. We were true fans; we cheered the close games, longed for a championship. Still, we knew that we were watching two simultaneous shows: LSU's and Pete's. In our hearts, we knew the team was not national caliber. In our hearts, we didn't care. Our ecstasy was here and now, in this drafty old barn . . . ecstasy achieved through one more behind-the-back pass, or fast break, or jump shot from so deep in the corner that the ball arrived from *behind* the backboard to fall soundlessly through the stunned net, everyone turning to a neighbor: *Did you see that?* The words became choral responses when repeated enough times: Did you see that? Did you see that?

And a piece of iconography fixed forever in our minds: at the top of his shot, just after release, his arms outstretched before him, Pete leaning back ten degrees from the vertical, a shock of hair thrown forward, individual sweat droplets glistening in the light around his face like an aura. During his senior year, LSU went 20-8 and won two games in the NIT Tournament in Madison Square Garden. But Al McGuire's Marquette team dispatched LSU 101-79, and the era came to a close. Pete Maravich never won a college championship; never won a pro championship either.

The photographs of Pete ten years later when his pro career came to an end are terrifying to look at. The eyes of an old man, despairing, burned-out, past caring. An old man at thirty-three. His Sonny Bono mustache made him look like a racetrack tout. We had used him up, consumed him, devoured him, and left nothing but a husk. Used him to slake our need, our appetite for the illustrious—we'd been doing so ever since he was an undersized thirteen-year-old in South Carolina, through high school, through the LSU years, the pro years, the years of alcohol abuse, depression, shredded knees, vegetarianism, UFOs, Bell's palsy, thoughts of suicide, his mother's alcoholism, her suicide, his father's death. At the autopsy, after Pete died suddenly at age forty, the doctors discovered a congenital heart defect. He should have died as a teenager with such a rare condition.

The exact opposite of other athletic prodigies born with freakishly supra-normal cardiovascular systems.

Toward the end of his life, though, he found peace—everyone agrees on this—in the love of his wife and sons, in God. God took His time, though, getting around to Pete. Was it necessary to have kept him waiting that long? To have let him wander down so many dark paths, alone, floundering, lost, used up by the game, used up by us?

The pro career lasted ten years—Hawks, Jazz, Celtics. Validated with the predictable All-Star selections, and 50th Anniversary All-Time Team, and retired jerseys, and 68 points scored against the Knicks in 1977. But for those of us who saw him at LSU, the pro career was almost meaningless, a sad second act.

Doubtless, we are prisoners of our own nostalgia: it is our own youths we mourn—to be eighteen, nineteen, twenty, on a winter night in Baton Rouge. Nothing to be too proud of here, psychologically, on our parts. And yet . . . to hell with wisdom and maturity. For a few of us lucky ones, there were three seasons long ago when you joined a throng on Highland Road and made your way three hours early to see a mere basketball game, and your brother was at your side, and the show began, your lungs burned, *the joy simply everywhere!* Words didn't need to be spoken, just a look, fleeting, between two brothers: *Did you see that?*

The Movie Theater: A Dream

The Usher: Wielding a flashlight, she prowls the aisles in search of transgressors—gum-chewers and talkers mostly—although plenty of amorous teens, drunks, and at least one actual bank robber (a farm boy, it turned out, with a take of $147) have, at one time or another, been interdicted and hauled off to a local version of the stocks or re-education camp or confessional. She's dressed in penal brown—brown skirt, brown jacket, brown shoes. Over the years, a deep apostolic disapproval has been conjoined in her to an alert, calmly competent nose for wrongdoing. She's no longer even shocked, having seen everything: the brawling young men, the children throwing up in the balcony, church groups filing in for *The Ten Commandments*, Cub Scouts running riot during *The Shaggy Dog*, the mayor having his heart attack, the fifteen-year-old giving birth to a strapping, ridiculously healthy baby girl in the ladies room during *Roman Holiday*, the moment of birth occurring precisely when Gregory Peck pulls his hand out of the Mouth of Truth (*la Bocca della Verità*) and scares Audrey Hepburn and she screams—the film-scream drowning out both young Effie's final push and the baby's first lusty yelp—the baby now wriggling in the arms of the stone-faced usher, who has already phoned the hospital, who will stay afterwards to clean things up, and who will lock up when the last straggler has been run out, after the last showing, in order to go home to her husband and her wood-frame house—this gray, competent usher who at the end of it all still disapproves of the movies she barely knows the titles of, of the foolish, too easily entertained public, of the cheap treats and Cokes they consume, of their infantile hopes, passions, fears—the corners of her mouth permanently turned down in quiet disapprobation of it all.

Artifacts: Why a pipe organ? Why a proscenium arch? Why brocaded curtains? Why box seats? Civilians never see the interior of the theater in full light. As well they shouldn't. A delicate business, that of theater preservation: the tattered stage curtain (its bottom-fringe moth-eaten), the mezzanine seats with their wilted doilies, the marble medallion above the screen, Tragedy and Comedy, imported from Carrara, but Comedy has lost his nose. The theater was once an opera house. Opened 1920. A small Southern town's vision of itself, its dream of higher things: born when a lumber broker, who had become a city magistrate, then street commissioner, then impresario, returned from a trip to Atlanta, and met with four of his cronies, fellow businessmen, fellow dreamers, who agreed to form a corporation, then to engage a St. Louis architecture firm, specialists in theater design and construction. A month later, a representative arrived on the Illinois Central, booked rooms in the Rudolpho Hotel, spread out on a dinner table his watercolor illustrations and sample books. He had already taken in the sights of the town, studied its hotels, streetcars, clothiers, environs, and, at the end of the evening, proposed a four-hundred-seat building and a modest range of ornamentation. The next day, it was the five partners themselves who decided on a corner lot downtown, twelve hundred seats, and an Italianate design (one of them, the lumber broker's best friend, had lived in New York for a year and had seen Caruso at the Metropolitan). Then, the five chose from the same sample books and watercolors the precise size, style, and number of wall sconces, pilasters, crystal chandeliers, side bays, and niches, even the velvet ropes in the lobby and the statue of Apollo—all of which turned out to cost almost exactly 34 percent more than the bank and mortgagees and holders of financial paper had allowed, had planned on, even taking into account an inevitable inflation of civic desire. And thus, after three years of vaudeville shows and touring Shakespeare companies (and one opera performance), the partners declared insolvency, and a movie chain bought the building, installed a thirty-foot-wide screen and two projectors and a Kimball organ and some additional fireproofing, and left everything else as they found it, the angels and chariots, candelabra and gold leaf. The old aspiration and dream of the opera house could still be experienced by audience-members, although, year by year, it was less noted, less remarked, except by a few grandmothers and great-aunts. The rest of us took our seats with far different expectations and dreams than those of the dead lumber broker and his friends. What would *they* have thought of the flickering light streaming above us? Such a strange light, which is born above and behind us, and which contains living beings—cowboys and gangsters, blondes and bullfighters. A beam that steadily widens and expands, then somehow reassembles itself at the last moment and becomes the movie we gaze upon.

The Ticket Booth: The terrible loneliness of the ticket booth lady . . . A hidden, slender door leads to her vertical coffin which stands alone, outside, two feet from the sidewalk, nearly in the street. What if a car jumped the curb? It happened a few years ago, she remembers, in Shreveport or Jackson, killing the employee, a twenty-year-old college student and newlywed. And the men. Where do they get the gall? The ticket lady is not a cocktail waitress, not a New Orleans B-girl, there to chat you up for a dollar. Teenage boys are worst of all. This is why the ticket lady is a lookalike of the usher—middle-aged, angular, impervious. Her attention turned mostly to the hard wooden stool she has to sit on all day; she'll end up a cripple sure enough. And the dinky little electric heater they give her in winter—thus her customary garb of sweaters and wool skirts and lap blanket, socks even, why not? No one can see down there. In the summer, the theater is air-conditioned but not the ticket booth. One year, they installed a little fan like the ones bus drivers have. It was broken by July and no one offered to buy a replacement. Perforated tickets come in one-thousand count rolls, six rolls to a box, arriving twice a year from a commercial arcade-and-amusement-park supplier in Cincinnati, a city better known for the manufacture of cash registers and billiard tables—exactly the kind of cold, efficient Northern city Ignatius J. Reilly always associated with machine parts and industrial repair. Ignatius, who idled away countless hours in New Orleans' movie houses, dispatching box after box of popcorn, offering commentary to anyone within earshot. The ticket lady pays no mind to the colors—yellow, blue, mauve, and green. She simply picks up a new roll from a closet next to the concession stand, carries it outdoors to her booth, and inserts it in the dispenser under her narrow countertop. Wrinkled bills pass across the slot at the bottom of her glass screen; a ticket slips out of the dispenser's metal lip—ADMIT ONE—along with a few nickels and quarters in change and the customer receives the chariot race in *Ben-Hur* . . . or Burt Lancaster in *Elmer Gantry*, coldcocking the pimp who just slapped Shirley Jones, "Don't you know that hurts?" Or Bogart, in *The Big Sleep*, visiting old General Sternwood in the greenhouse, taking his jacket off, having a brandy. Or transcendence itself!—Grace Kelly, Ingrid Bergman, Audrey Hepburn . . .

The Staircase: A second balcony exists at the extreme rear of the theater, separated from the principal balcony by a sturdy low wall. This is where African Americans sit—during a four-and-a half-decade period, 1920–1964—from the opening of the opera house until the passage of the Civil Rights Act. This second balcony is obtained by a private staircase and a private entrance. From the street, the narrow unmarked entryway is nearly invisible, stands just to the right of the theater's outdoor foyer—a plain wooden door between the theater proper and a jewelry store next door. Inside, a theater employee collects the same admission price as white customers pay at the ticket booth, although no tickets are needed here, customers are sent straight up a set of spiral stairs to the balcony. There is no concession stand here, no bathroom, no lobby. Once seated in the three rows of the second balcony, patrons abstain from loud outbursts, from too much laughter, from drawing attention to themselves. There is no interchange whatsoever between this mute, invisible gallery pressed against the extreme rear of the auditorium and the rest of the theatergoers (myself, my family, neighbors, fellow citizens), who successfully ignore the second balcony, don't see it, have learned to abstract it nearly out of existence. Forty-four years.

Lucre: Not the lobby floor, which is marble terrazzo—and indestructible. Not the sidewalk outside, which is concrete. But the auditorium floor, a wall-to-wall expanse of red oak. Burnished to a dark, winey bronze by ten thousand cleanings and rewaxings. And by the endless mopping of Coke spills, endless sweeping up of popcorn, candy, and candy wrappers. One-inch-thick oak is as hard as steel—but it is not intended for so many assaults by wet mops; and thus, slight cracks appear from time to time, from contraction and expansion of the wood, which is, after all, a living thing. Cracks through which coins are said to disappear, from purses, pocketbooks, unmended trousers, from those small coin purses businessmen carry, of green and blue fabric with small brass snaps. And so, as the legend goes—there's a fortune there, beneath the theater, unseen, unobtainable, known only to mice, raccoons, an occasional opossum—a legend we both believe and don't believe. Enough buried treasure to restore the gold leaf and dreams of the old opera house of 1920, all those nickels and dimes and pennies slowing sinking into damp earth, returning to ore.

The Projectionist: His two constant threats: deafness and sleep. He is unmarried. Nameless, gaunt, taller than expected, a graying, un-aging boy somewhere between forty-seven and sixty-seven. Said to live in an apartment downtown, only a block from the theater, above a department store, one of those windows you glance at once or twice a year, painted black or advertising a dentist's office. But he might actually live in the theater, in his perilous aerie, which no one visits, not the usher, nor the ticket lady, nor the manager, nor the frail, nonagenarian absentee theater-owner himself (who bought the business from the Loews chain in 1941), who is the projectionist's distant relative and benefactor, nor the United States Postal Service employee who hand-delivers the heavy two-reel film cans once a week, conveyed upstairs by a dumbwaiter.

His is a perfectly timed ballet: the changing of the reels. His partners, the two 35mm projectors—matched 1951 Gaumont-Kalees, English-made, the size of refrigerators, indestructible, near silent (hearing loss is a professional hazard for projectionists—the ceaseless whirr of reel-sprockets), their cast-iron bases bolted in place with one-and-three-quarter inch steel anchors to steel foundations, the load transferred downward by columns (he saw all this once during remodeling) straight onto concrete pads beneath the building itself.

And the movies? The voluptuous stories he engenders?

He never watches them. They are of no interest. For him, they are only a blur of enormous faces and cheekbones; the screech of auto tires and violins. His attention is elsewhere, in his tiny workroom—cue-marks, carbon arc lamps, shutter-gates, rectifiers, RCA sound heads. A life of precision, of relentless, unmoving time.

Exterior Shot: A cold, rainy night downtown, the narrow streets clean and slick—these are winter rains, which are said to have "set in"—calm, patient, enduring. An enormous, three-sided marquee projects over the sidewalk like the prow of a ship. It glows with red, blue, green, and orange neon lights. White letters of movie titles and stars' names. Another neon sign—vertical, thirty feet tall—with the theater's name rises above the marquee, attached to the limestone building itself. The theater is a solid four-story rectangular building, on a corner lot, its facade and cornices embellished with stonework and capitals; a series of urnlike decorations line the rooftop. Maybe the theater *is* a ship, ablaze in the night, lighting up the whole block with its urgent communiqué: NOW PLAYING. The streets are awash in light, so much light that the whole town is transformed (or so we believe). Twelve glass display cases—eight protected by the marquee and foyer, four out on the sidewalk, naked to the elements. Exaggerated, brightly colored posters and the faces we identify with a glance—Doris, Rock, Bing, Gregory. Row after row of tiny light bulbs outline every poster and sign (who changes the bulbs when they go out? Do they ever go out?). Then, at the far right of the entrance: Why a bicycle rack? Why are there two blue Schwinns here at this late hour? This outdoor antechamber exists for us to mingle in, while we wait for the ticket line to thin down. Cars stop, women get out, stepping over shiny puddles, brightness of laughter, satin gowns, coats and ties.

All this light enlarges us. We believe so above everything. Because we have seen them—the faraway movie palaces of the cities, theaters which are even grander than our own. (Their names are exotic, barely conceivable—Moorish, Spanish Colonial, French Renaissance, Tudor Revival, Egyptian, Beaux Arts, Art Deco, Art Nouveau, Art Moderne.) If we wanted to, we could travel to them on the train, to Jackson, Mississippi, then north to Memphis, Chicago, New York, each step a progression upward, yes, but also a link—if we can touch such greatness, then we partake of greatness, our existence is confirmed. (The secret fear of small-town residents is that we do not exist.) And why are we so sure that those distant theaters are really there—those dreams, visions, hyper-realities? Because we've seen them in the movies.

1974: Razed for a street overpass.

1964

They could be in Cuba.

– Mississippi Gov. Paul Johnson

You know, those boys may have decided to go up North or someplace and have a short vacation. They'll probably be coming back shortly.

– Neshoba County Attorney Rayford Jones

Philadelphia – from Gk., lit. "brotherly love," from *philos* "loving" + *adelphos* "brother."

– *Online Etymology Dictionary*. Douglas Harper, Historian

On the afternoon of June 21, 1964, three young men drove a blue Ford Fairlane station wagon toward the small town of Philadelphia, Mississippi. They were civil rights workers—two of them were white; one was African American. Their names were Michael Schwerner, Andrew Goodman, and James Chaney, and they were shot to death later that night by Ku Klux Klansmen.

Forty-five years have passed since that June Sunday, and millions of Americans born since then probably wouldn't recognize the three men's names if asked to pick them out of a list—this, even though dozens of books and articles have been written about them, two Hollywood films have been based on their murders, and their names are part of the iconography of the civil rights era.

Those same millions of Americans might not be able to imagine the existence of a national apartheid—the South—an American repressive state, fully armed and lawfully instituted, flourishing in the twentieth century. Even for those of us who were living then, some of the details have begun to blur, the memories to fade.

As the historian Howard Ball tells us, after the 1954 Supreme Court decision of *Brown v. Board of Education of Topeka, Kansas*, the white South believed itself to be besieged, believed its traditional "way of life" (namely, segregation and white supremacy) was in danger of passing from the land; and then set about with every power at hand to fight anyone or anything that opposed it. The ferocity of Southern resistance was not limited to Klansmen or other extremists, but was taken up by governors, senators, congressmen, state legislatures, judges, newspapers, White Citizens Councils, all. It was in the face of this overwhelming apparatus of state power (abetted by the Klan's terrorism) that civil rights workers like Schwerner, Chaney, and Goodman risked their lives.

The campaign of 1964 was called Freedom Summer—it was to be a voter registration drive staffed by over a thousand young volunteers, mostly white Northern college students, both men and women. Of the volunteers who came to Mississippi that summer, most knew that in the 1960s the state held first place among all Southern states in a number of dismal statistics. In his book, *Freedom Summer*, Doug McAdam gathers page after page of these grim numbers:

> Median nonwhite family income averaged just \$1,444 in 1960, lowest in the United States, and barely a third of the average for Mississippi whites.
>
> Consider that in 1964 the average state expenditure for education was just \$21.77 per black pupil as compared to \$81.86 for every white pupil.

> As of 1960, [black] infant mortality rates continued to run two times higher than the rate for Mississippi whites and nearly 250 percent higher than the national average for whites.
>
> Nowhere were racial restrictions on voter registration more zealously applied. The result was by far the lowest rate of black registration in the South—6.7 percent—and a number of interesting anomalies. For instance in 1962 there were five counties in the state with black majorities and yet not a single black registrant.

Those college volunteers—who were mostly in their twenties, idealistic, politically progressive, and perhaps overly-innocent—believed that spending their summer in the South in 1964 was a way of taking a stand for justice, for freedom, and for equality. But they may not have understood just how many white Southerners believed the exact opposite.

In their comprehensive history of the murders, *We Are Not Afraid*, authors Seth Cagin and Philip Dray lead us step by step through the events of that summer. After the three young men were murdered that Sunday, their bodies were transported to a nearby farm and buried under a dam; then the station wagon was driven to a swamp and torched. The Klansmen used gasoline to ignite the vehicle, not dynamite (a favorite weapon in their arsenal), since the wagon wasn't destroyed, simply burned from the inside out. After which, the murderers made a critical mistake: they left the station wagon visible in Bogue Chitto swamp. The original plan was to drive it to Alabama, not leave it in Neshoba County. Perhaps their idea was to give it a good shove, a roll, into the swamp, where it might reasonably be expected to sink in the muck, or disappear in the undergrowth like a rock thrown into tall grass. If it didn't disappear entirely, perhaps it wouldn't be found for a year or two, by which time the whole business might have blown over.

The Klansmen wanted especially to kill Michael Schwerner, aged twenty-four—"Goatee" was their codename for him. Schwerner was a New Yorker, a Jew, a Congress of Racial Equality (CORE) staff member. The other two men were not primary targets; they just happened to be there that Sunday: James Chaney, twenty-one, who was black, a local man from Meridian; and Andrew Goodman, twenty, from New York. Did the conspirators know that Goodman was a Jew also? Maybe not, he'd only arrived the day before. Schwerner, though, they knew very well; they'd been following him for months from his base in Meridian. Schwerner was married at the time—to a woman from New York, also Jewish, but she was in Ohio that Sunday. The Klansmen must have thought it fitting that so many Northern Jews had come south to Mississippi—all in accordance with the rallies, with the talks and the speeches that they'd been listening to for months. In the vocabulary of Klan dementia, a kind of ultimate spiritual war had come to pass between the forces of white Christian purity and the forces of evil—evil made visible in Jews, Communists, atheists, blacks, and almost any other non-Anglo-Saxon. And all of it had come to a head in 1964, in the South. It was as if someone had drawn a line in the dirt, and said: Here . . . here is your choice. Step over to this side with the patriots and believers and defenders of freedom . . . or do nothing, sit on the sidelines while a great fire of history enkindles, comes to life around you.

Still, they followed regulations. The death sentence had come down from their superior, Sam Bowers in Laurel, the state Imperial Wizard. The order was specific: eliminate Goatee. When Edgar Ray Killen, the Neshoba County kleagle, received the order from Bowers, surveillance was increased and the rough outline of a plan was drawn up. In what was doubtless a ploy to lure Schwerner into Neshoba County, the Klan first attacked a rural black church, Mount Zion Methodist Church, in Longdale, on the night of June 16, assaulting some of its members, then torching the little church, burning it to the ground. The Klansmen believed (correctly as it turned out) that Schwerner wouldn't be able to resist driving from Meridian to Longdale in order to see the ruins and take statements from church members. It was then only a matter of waiting for the right moment—a moment which occurred on June 21 when the station wagon appeared in the county and was spotted by one of the conspirators.

In fact, the station wagon was stopped twice during the course of the murders—a series of events which turned out to be a prolonged, highly complicated operation. The three men were stopped the first time for speeding by a Neshoba County deputy. Then they were held in jail for several hours; and released from jail around 10:30 p.m., given the keys to their vehicle and told to leave town. It was during this second occurrence—when they were leaving Philadelphia late Sunday night—that they were stopped by three cars of Klansmen on a dark country road.

Perhaps we have no right to speculate about the mental states of the three young men that Sunday—ordinary human beings in unspeakable duress. No right to concoct an interior monologue. But it is hard not to imagine that James Chaney understood the danger more readily than the other two. Chaney was a native, had grown up in that part of the state.

Michael Schwerner had few illusions either, knew full well the possibilities—he and his wife had been in Meridian for several months; he'd already seen the inside of a jail cell. Andrew Goodman had just arrived from Ohio, from the Freedom Summer training center, and he too claimed that he was no child, no innocent.

But Chaney was born there. His blood quickened by generations of habitation in the South, by the interminable summers, mosquitoes, woods, towns, desolate two-lane blacktop roads like Highway 16 on a Sunday afternoon, the red blinking light pulling them over, the deputy writing a speeding ticket, saying, "Come with me." When Chaney saw (not looked into; he wouldn't have stared long into such a visage) the soft-lidded, pasty face of Deputy Cecil Ray Price, it's probable that he knew in that one instant that he was dead, that he would be dead by the end of the day, even if a few hours had to pass, even if there was a pantomime of officialese and arrest and jail-time that had to be gotten through, before the various forces could align themselves for the actual killings. It's probable that he knew it long before Schwerner and Goodman, who, no matter what they had seen, read, experienced, imagined, about such a place as Philadelphia—couldn't really know, as Chaney could.

A murder conspiracy gains several rather obvious advantages when the sheriff and deputy of the county are themselves members of the conspiracy. Neshoba County Sheriff Lawrence Rainey, and his deputy, Cecil Price, were both said to be members of the local klavern, were both personable, smiling officers, caricatures of small-town Southern lawmen: Stetson-wearing, well-armed, tobacco-chewing, lethal. (Rainey had previously killed one, possibly two, black men *in the line of duty.*) If you were casting their parts in Hollywood, you'd reject one actor after another as excessively stereotypical. But the real Rainey and Price strode right through the caricatures all the way to the other side, drawling, smiling, lying, as if they already knew about the Hollywood casting agent, and knew that they could outlast anyone—the FBI, the Yankee journalists, the NAACP, and the other outsiders—if they simply held their course, kept moving forward, admitted nothing. They appear in numerous photographs in 1964, in uniform or out, beefy and round-faced. Deputy Price even appears in one photo (no paid actor could have pulled off *that* performance) while helping to carry one of the three plastic-encased corpses—his countenance is solemn, dutiful, responsible—as if he were just doing his job in the ordinary course of Neshoba County business.

Price was twenty-six-years-old in 1964. Only twenty-six, and on his own that Sunday—the sheriff was out of the office all day, the very day the blue station wagon motored past him on Highway 16, east of Philadelphia, headed into town.

Price spun his patrol car around and gave chase. The station wagon was not speeding, but such a technicality wouldn't be anything to worry greatly about. He could always stop them for suspicious activity or for "investigation" of suspicious activity or for, well, anything. But it was highly convenient when Chaney, Schwerner, and Goodman drove into the Philadelphia city limits and failed to slow down to thirty-five miles per hour. Now the arrest was legal.

By 1964, the South's days of open-air lynchings were long past. No longer could a Klansman like Deputy Price simply empty his service revolver into three undesirables on the side of the road in broad daylight. At least not in front of the First Methodist Church. Nor could he hand them straight over to his colleagues, other patriots and ministers of justice, to be hanged from the first oak tree they saw, the bodies left to rot as a warning, a symbol of retribution and judgment. Price needed two things after he arrived with the prisoners in the Neshoba County jail—time to contact Edgar Ray Killen and plausible deniability for himself.

But first, he had to get the prisoners processed, and safely locked in the cells. Then, he had to make sure that they made no phone calls; or, if anyone called to inquire about them, make sure no information went out. No doubt, he found a way to keep old Mr. and Mrs. Herring busy—the married couple who ran the jail.

The hours passed quickly—there were many details for Price and Killen to iron out. Soon, it was ten, ten-thirty at night. Time to release the prisoners, time for the rest of Killen's plan to unfold.

Price's role was to tail the station wagon for a few miles out of Philadelphia, until time to make the pass-off; and, then, if something didn't seem right, he could hit the lights again, re-arrest them, then turn them over to Killen's boys and then head back to town . . . Which is exactly what he did.

Oddly enough, that year's version of the Mississippi Klan, the White Knights, had only recently been formed in February 1964 as a response to the civil rights incursions of the previous year and the well-publicized, upcoming Freedom Summer. Between the 1920s and 1964, strange as it sounds, the Klan in Mississippi had lain fallow, offering white citizens of the era the opportunity for a strange kind of pride in racist self-containment. Cagin and Dray explain:

> Mississippians in May 1961 still had sufficient confidence in the state's established institutions to meet the integrationist threat. The Ku Klux Klan had never been as strong in Mississippi as it was elsewhere in the South for the simple reason that given the strident racism built into Mississippi government at the state, county, and local levels, there was no need for an alternative vigilante force to protect "the southern way of life."

There was no need . . . At times, the acts of hatred and injustice were so layered one upon the other that things toppled over into the surreal. In 1962, Bill Higgs, a white civil rights lawyer from Jackson ran across "an 'overlooked' black Freedom Rider from Los Angeles languishing in the Clarksdale jail. The rider, law student Dewey Peterson, had been arrested during the summer of 1961 in an attempt to integrate the Clarksdale bus depot and had been held incommunicado for nearly a year." (Cagin and Dray)

In 1964, in Philadelphia, a long jail stretch was not one of the options under consideration. The options carried out were these: Michael Schwerner was killed by a gunshot to the chest; Andrew Goodman, also by a gunshot to the chest; James Chaney, by multiple gunshots.

When the shootings were over, the Klansmen gathered up their spent cartridges, then stuffed the bodies into the back of the station wagon and drove to the burial site. A bulldozer was waiting for them; plus a bulldozer driver. A few more hours of work were necessary—the dam had to be rebuilt, everything had to be cleaned up, groomed, raked over.

And they almost got away with it. First, they used too many men. It doesn't take three vehicles and nine or so armed Klansmen to deal with three unarmed men (who were all slight of build, all under six feet tall) on Rock Cut Road in Neshoba County in the dead of night. Nor others roaming around town with first-hand information of the events—Olen Burrage, for example, owner of the earthen dam, and Herman Tucker, the bulldozer operator, and Sheriff Rainey and Killen and Bowers and the other field commanders.

Second, the station wagon, their biggest mistake. For some reason they gave that responsibility to Herman Tucker, not a sworn Klan member, not a principal in the murders. He was given orders to drive the car to Alabama and dispose of it there, but he abandoned it in Neshoba County a mere eighty feet off Highway 21. He didn't even remove the license plate. If he had taken the car to Alabama or Georgia, or almost anywhere, it could have been left in a gulley or at the bottom of a ravine and probably would have never been found. Or, as an alternative—many Klansmen are excellent mechanics—they could have dismantled the entire vehicle during the night and dropped the pieces in a hundred rivers and ponds all over the South.

If they hadn't botched the station wagon disposal, the bodies might still be there. It would have been as if Schwerner, Chaney, and Goodman had never existed, had vanished off the face of the earth. And such a task would not be a difficult one to accomplish in the thick forests, in the deep fastness of Neshoba County.

In August 1964, when the three bodies were finally discovered buried in the earthen dam, Neshoba County local historian, Florence Mars, said that no one in Philadelphia asked the question, "Who would have done such a thing?" Instead everyone asked, "Who told?" (Cagin and Dray)

Michael Schwerner's wife, Rita, was in Ohio at the training center when word came that the three men were missing. She immediately left for Mississippi, an act which itself was astounding in 1964—like entering a war zone. Reporters claim that she didn't intend to play the noble widow; and, indeed, she went straight to work, asking questions, confronting the governor and the Feds, pressing, pushing, causing problems everywhere she went. "I don't want sympathy," she responded to an envoy from President Johnson, "I want my husband back." On June 26, three days after the station wagon was found, and only five days after the murders, she went to Philadelphia itself, drove through the back roads of Neshoba County, was tailed for a time by a pickup truck, and barely escaped a roadblock of backwoods vigilantes. (The whole thing could have happened all over again!) In Philadelphia, she confronted a scandalized and belligerent Sheriff Rainey, then viewed the burned-out car. She wouldn't leave until seeing the car for herself.

There are a number of photographs of her during those days. In one, she is seated on some kind of sofa or banquette in a waiting room or office or motel room. The wall behind her is made of cinderblock, institutional. There's a tiny Formica shelf or table at her side, with a soda bottle, a water glass, a pack of cigarettes, and an ash tray. She's wearing sunglasses, her right hand touching her face. She is only five feet tall, waifish, her dark hair done up anyhow, bare arms, a simple cotton shift.

Among her first public words: "I suggest that if Mr. Chaney, a native Negro Mississippian, had been alone at the time of the disappearance, this case, like many before it, would have gone unnoticed."

The unspoken but obvious truth. But unnerving to hear such words coming from the wife of one of the men so recently killed. And a truth that she has never shied from repeating, even today, forty-five years later. To speak such words in 1964, in the very first hours of shock and grief and horror—it is hard to imagine such a reserve of integrity from a tiny, frail young woman (twenty-two-years-old), amid the offered hatred, amid the smell of a charred car-interior and such a cast of grotesques.

During the FBI manhunt, between June 23, the date of the station wagon's discovery, and August 4, the day of the earthen dam, other unsought corpses began turning up in Mississippi. First, a floating black torso near Natchez (the lower half of a man); then a second one near the Pearl River. In the Big Black River, the corpse of a boy about fourteen was found, identification never made. All told, a busy year for the Klan.

> By summer's end . . . thirty-five shootings (six black civil rights workers were killed between January and May 1964 while planning the summer project); Schwerner, Chaney, and Goodman murdered in June; four others wounded; thirty black home bombings; thirty-seven churches burned; more than 1,000 Freedom Summer students arrested; at least eighty beatings of black and white civil rights workers, by white mobs and racist police officers; and untold numbers of harassing and threatening telephone calls. (Howard Ball, *Murder in Mississippi*)

In 2002, the novelist Donald E. Westlake dedicated one of his books to "My old friend Mickey Schwerner, who was murdered with James Chaney and Andy Goodman on a berm in Mississippi the night of June 21, 1964 . . ."

Westlake, who was born in Brooklyn in 1933, must have known Schwerner when they were both young men in New York.

There's a strange shock in reading Westlake's words, a dizziness in realizing that Michael Schwerner was—well, someone's friend, not simply a civil rights martyr and icon, not simply a name forever married to Philadelphia, Mississippi, to a blue station wagon and an earthen dam.

A shock to think of Schwerner as a young man *before* Mississippi. To think of him, of Andrew Goodman and James Chaney, the three of them as ordinary men and boys, who had friends, held jobs, went to school, chased girls, bummed cigarettes . . . *My old friend Mickey.*

In his own brief twenty years, Andy Goodman graduated from the Walden School in New York City, spent a semester at University of Wisconsin-Madison, attended Queen's College in New York, did some acting off-Broadway, fell in love, did construction work, rode the bus to West Virginia to view Appalachian poverty firsthand as a seventeen-year-old, took part in protests at the 1964 World's Fair.

James (J.E.) Chaney grew up in 1940s Mississippi as the second oldest of five children. His mother earned $1.50 a day as a housekeeper in white homes. His inherited universe—apartheid in its most rigorous form, a negative image of Andy Goodman's Upper West Side. He tried escaping Meridian via the Army but was classified 4-F due to asthma. Began working with his father as a plasterer on construction jobs. Traveled the South from job to job, but always returned to Meridian, his hometown. By chance, J.E. met a CORE activist from New Orleans, liked what he saw, and was recruited as an early CORE member in Meridian, becoming the staff driver, guide, source of local knowledge. In CORE, he found his vocation, his life's work.

Mickey and Rita Schwerner were married in June 1962 in New York—the two of them, already at ages twenty and nineteen, committed activists, preternaturally political and single-minded. Yet

Mickey was also a personable friend, teacher, mentor, a cut-up, a rock 'n' roller, who grew up in New York state with an older brother in a boys' world of baseball, tennis, golf, football.

It is this ordinariness that is hinted at in Westlake's laconic phrase.

Because the three didn't seek to be martyrs. Yes, they were attempting an impossible work, under horrific circumstances, propelled by a courage seldom met in twenty-year-olds, then or now, but their lives are not reducible to three photographs on an FBI Missing Poster, names learned by rote for our martyrology. They were three young men who drove to Neshoba County that Sunday to view a burned-down black church, and to interview a few church members, some of whom had been severely beaten, to take statements, to make plans for the coming week, to make plans to speak to the FBI and the Justice Department about Mount Zion Church when they got back to Meridian, their home base, forty-five minutes away. Doubtless they were talking among themselves on the ride back, with the energy of the young, outraged by what they'd seen, but, being young, they were mostly looking to the future, thinking of tomorrow, Monday, when they could begin making phone calls, begin to get something accomplished. Deputy Price's patrol car passed them a few miles east of Philadelphia.

In 1967, eighteen Klansmen were tried in Federal Court for conspiracy to deprive Schwerner, Goodman, and Chaney of their civil rights. (A state murder indictment was not even attempted.) Only seven of the eighteen were found guilty—Sheriff Rainey was among those acquitted. Longest sentence imposed—ten years. Most of those convicted received either six or three-year sentences. Deputy Price served four years of his six-year sentence, then returned home to Philadelphia, where he worked as a truck driver, surveyor, jewelry store repairman, joined the country club, and was elected vice-president of the Neshoba County Shriners.

In 2005, forty-one years after the deaths, a jury failed to convict head conspirator Edgar Ray Killen of murder, although he was found guilty of the lesser charge of manslaughter.

To date, the State of Mississippi has convicted no one for murder in the deaths of James Chaney, Andrew Goodman, and Michael Schwerner.

2

WRITERS, CHARACTERS, STRATAGEMS

The Best Southern Short Story Ever?

Without ever leaving her hide-out in Milledgeville, Georgia, Flannery O'Connor knew all there was to know about the two-lane, dirt and blacktop Southern roads of the 1950s—with their junkyards and tourist courts, gravel pits and pine trees that pressed at the edges of the road. She knew the slogans of the Burma Shave signs, knew the names of barbecue joints and the chicken baskets on their menus. She also knew a backwoods American cadence and vocabulary you'd think was limited to cops, truckers, runaway teens, and patrons of the Teardrop Inn, where at midnight somebody could always be counted on to go out to a pickup truck and come back with a shotgun. She was a virtuoso mimic, and she assimilated whole populations of American sounds and voices, and then offered them back to us from time to time in her small fictional detonations, one of which she named, in 1953, "A Good Man Is Hard to Find."

The plot is sewn together through a devious coincidence. While planning a car trip to Florida, a Georgia family (grandmother, son, wife, three children) learns that an escaped criminal named The Misfit is roaming about the region. The family embarks anyway, stops for lunch at a country restaurant, has a car accident, and is slaughtered by The Misfit and his two cohorts.

In a characteristic sleight of hand, O'Connor decided to give the story to the grandmother, a pint-sized heroine for this little tale of mayhem and death. The grandmother (that's her name in the story) appears in every scene and speaks nearly all of the dialogue, rivaled only by the two menacing, boisterous older children and an unexpected visitor in the final scene. She takes control of things from the outset—wheedling, conniving, whining, and manipulating the entire family to go along with her plans. She's a self-pitying narcissist, a megalomaniacal, self-delighting tyrant of her little middle-class family. She utters clichés day and night and considers herself, in the end, always a proper lady:

> I wouldn't take my children in any direction with a criminal like that aloose in it. I couldn't answer to my conscience if I did.

> In my time, children were more respectful of their native states and their parents and everything else.

> People are certainly not nice like they used to be.

And naturally, it is the grandmother's hiding of her cat in the car's back seat (couldn't bear leaving Pitty Sing home alone) and her maneuvers to visit a roadside attraction that lead to the car accident and the family's destruction.

In the final scene, the grandmother meets her narcissistic match, who just happens to be a sociopathic killer. The duet that plays between her and The Misfit is a pinnacle of American comic writing—a dizzying dialogue that takes place at the same time as the gunshot murders of two adults, two children, and an infant. Like a pair of theological vaudevillians, they speak of Christ, fate, good and evil, and the workings out of their respective salvation. For the first time in her life, the grandmother is nearly dumb with terror, reduced to stammering out pleas for her life. The middle-aged Misfit, almost scholarly in his spectacles, recounts his horrific life—he is at once ominous and detached, despairing and alert, a kind of proselytizing anti-prophet, utterly given over to impulse and violence, and who, in spite of or perhaps because of the completeness of his solipsism, speaks one or two words of unwitting truth—truth that, improbably enough, sets the old woman free.

Along with the grandmother, everyone in the story speaks in banalities—the children, John Wesley and June Star, the garrulous restaurateur Red Sammy, The Misfit's two henchmen, Hiram and Bobby Lee—in short, everyone in the story, including The Misfit (perhaps especially The Misfit), although his language also manages to be complex and self-aware. With The Misfit, the reader is jerked out of an impatient restlessness and distaste for these tiresome people. He's the only charismatic figure in the story, and his compressed life story has the cadence and richness of a poem:

> I was a gospel singer for a while. I been most everything. Been in the arm service, both land and sea, at home and abroad, been twict married, been an undertaker, been with the railroads, plowed Mother Earth, been in a tornado . . .

In one sense, The Misfit is a co-hero of the story, as significant as the grandmother—a hypnotic, dazzling Iago, of sorts. But O'Connor is doing a number on us with the magnetic Misfit, has intentionally made him the only interesting character in the story, so that we would be drawn to him for a time, so that we would be curious about him, half believe him. Indeed, we're spellbound, laughing, wincing, at his delicious language—all until the moment that he reminds us of his horrific potential.

The Shakespeare critic A.C. Bradley once said that the first thing to keep in mind about Iago is that you can't believe a single word he says. You have to distrust everything. Certainly, the same holds for The Misfit, who, like his predecessor, is so penetrated with untruth that he lies before he thinks, lies as he breathes. He's in that great line of backwoods con men—quite capable of rewriting his charismatic life story on every ditchbank in Georgia, and the Biblical language he is so fluent in is just another form of his con.

The story, which had begun as a cartoon, a comedy of '50s manners, has taken, in a handful of pages, a remarkable turn. All the events have occurred in a single day, during this balmy summer car trip in rural Georgia. There is no chance that a reader should accept O'Connor's plot—with its blatantly placed clue in the first paragraph. Yet she makes it work. We laugh our way through a brief series of scenes, ride along in the crowded car, have lunch at Red Sammy's, get lost on the dirt road, laugh again when Pitty Sing (who, it must be said, had been quite well behaved for most of the trip) jumps on the son's shoulder and causes the wreck; and then somehow, not quite knowing how it has happened, we find ourselves slumped in shock and terror alongside the doomed family at the bottom of a ditch, looking up at a cloudless sky and three men looming above.

The grandmother's son is named Bailey, but we never learn his wife's name. She is simply "the children's mother," anonymous, almost selfless in the grandmother's characteristic worldview. O'Connor makes her the butt of an early joke on page one, giving her a face "as broad and innocent as a cabbage." During the accident, she is thrown from the car, still holding the infant, and breaks her shoulder. She sits there, stiffening in shock, as her husband and young son are led away by The Misfit's henchmen, to be murdered in the woods. Soon, the murderers come for her, and The Misfit quietly asks her "to step off yonder with Bobby Lee and Hiram and join your husband."

Nearly mute in pain and horror, she can only say, "Yes, thank you." Then she takes the two remaining children and quietly walks off to her death. O'Connor, who had humiliated the young woman earlier, gives her back to us now in something close to tragedy, in a miraculous dignity; and her "Yes, thank you" becomes the most poignant moment of the story.

Only the grandmother remains. Grasping at straws, she mutters, "Jesus, Jesus," and The Misfit chimes right back in. And then in the midst of his philosophizing, he speaks the central line of the story: "Jesus thown everything off balance." We know that The Misfit is speaking out of his own insanity and violence, but O'Connor is stretching language so far here that, for a moment at least, the reality of these Georgia trees and skies starts to crack apart. We've been working our way through some of the strangest American prose ever written. Six people are dead. And The Misfit becomes the most memorable religious character in recent American fiction.

In the last moments of the story, the grandmother has reached the limits of despair. She alone is left alive. She has begged for her life, twisted and turned every way she knows, has reached some unspeakable point of horror and fear and catastrophe, and she cries out to The Misfit, "Why you're one of my babies. You're one of my own children!" Her entire atrocious, selfish, ignorant, useless life has led to this. And in its last moments, the improbable occurs. She breaks through, speaks words she doesn't even realize she is speaking. She reaches out to The Misfit and touches him on the shoulder—a common enough rural gesture. At her touch, The Misfit, a fully realized nihilist, shoots her dead.

The story runs quickly to its close. One or two more sentences. The Misfit tells Bobby Lee, "She would of been a good woman, if it had been somebody there to shoot her every minute of her life." It has taken the extremity of death for the grandmother to escape the shell of her egoism—a transformation that The Misfit, a shrewd psychologist, readily comprehends, even as he is the very agent of her destruction.

Thus, in the guise of a Deep South horror story, O'Connor gave American letters something else altogether: a religiously audacious work of literature, a spiritual puzzle—a small miracle.

Amid the Swirling Ghosts

In the spring of 1928, the author of *The Sound and the Fury* was a thirty-year-old bachelor, living at home with his parents in Oxford, Mississippi—the town freak, a Southern poet and limping cliché, little Billy Falkner (having changed his name as a would-be, laughably fraudulent RAF pilot), five feet, six inches tall, rejected by his first love who had married a lawyer, a better catch. Although he had published a couple of novels, his career was stalled. He was working at odd jobs, painting signs and houses. No money, no prospects, no future.

The expected result for such a Southern aesthete would ordinarily be some kind of tortured allegorical concoction, full of myths and Greek—but he'd already done *that*—in *The Marble Faun*, his vanity-press book of poems. Maybe he would rework the poems as a novel this time, a thrilling old style adventure and quest with plenty of murky isles, shepherds, and nymphs. Who could have predicted? Was he that different from all the other would-be novelists and poets in dozens of airless Southern towns? Or were they precursors of some sort? Perhaps it took all of them, their folly and pitiable waste, to add up somehow, by some weird literary arithmetic, to produce the one among them who would actually do it, create an enduring work of art.

And what was the source of the grief? For *The Sound and the Fury* is a kind of delirium and fantasia on the themes of grief and loss, an explosion of an elegy: "We have sold Benjy's pasture so that Quentin may go to Harvard . . ." Or does there have to be a single, identifiable occasion of loss for a man at that juncture, at that moment in a small town in the drear backwoods of the American South, a moment set firmly in the nineteenth century?

The piece is drenched in erotic frustration and impotence and rage, a whirlpool of sexual terror and dread; but why does its eruption of despair expand outward to cover virtually everything—women, family, parents, siblings, friends, townsfolk? Those Southerners!—haven't we heard all about them?—regionalists gone off their rockers. Still, there actually was a mentally handicapped townsman, pacing a fence two or three blocks away from his parents' house in Oxford; and an alcoholic father, violent, raging; and a grandmother, dying in some upstairs room in a Mississippi summer.

In any event, for the reader, first order of business is to get the two Quentins straight:

—male and female

—uncle and niece

—suicide and illegitimate daughter

The daughter's mother, the heroine of the story, was herself an outcast. Both women we soon learn (seventeen years apart) were addicted to assignations with town riffraff, as well as traveling salesmen, and sideshow barkers.

When you have the two Quentins straight, you can work on the male ancestry from Scotland, with a few more Quentins thrown in. Next the two Maurys—uncle (on the mother's side) and nephew.

But remember the nephew's name will change to Benjamin (Benjy) when he is a child. Now half a dozen Jasons. Read up on Scottish wars with England.

The book is divided into four sections, labeled by date, starting with a seemingly random April day in 1928. But why does the author go backwards to 1910 in the second section? Then in the third, why go simultaneously forward (or at least return) to 1928 and back, by one day? Then end everything one day after the first section (still in 1928), but two days after the preceding third section, and eighteen years after the second section. Got it? And then, for added fun, while inside any of the four sections, just jump the hell all over the place, amid another dozen or so time or place settings, using typescript changes to indicate a shift (sort of) but little else.

Once upon a time, four children lived with their parents in a house in the woods. Good. "Once upon a time." But right after "time," try switching gears to a first-person narrator, a young man, let's say—one of the four children, who is now grown up, twenty years old, having left the old home place and his siblings and his parents and moved to Boston; currently in a kind of odd mood, not too rational, a lot on his mind. So, right here, right after "time," let's let him talk for, say, one-hundred-thirty pages about how unhappy he is, a few problems he remembers about growing up, maybe some unresolved issues about his sense of self, about his alcoholic father, his self-pitying, neurasthenic mom, his screwing-everybody-in-town little sis. All the while throwing in a few dozen other characters, with multiple, overlapping names, incidents, memories, current(?) characters, and actions, even some dialogue for good measure (in the middle of his reverie) that may or may not be correctly remembered, or even factual (if, by this point, there is such a thing). Good. Go back to "Once upon a time, four children . . ." Back to the main story. Read as far as "four children," when we'll switch to the mind of a mentally handicapped man, thirty-three-years-old (or make that thirteen, or three or five or eighteen)—who, of course, cannot speak, but we'll let him speak anyway for ninety-two pages, and, for that matter, we'll even let other people speak (carry on conversations, etc.—useful to import additional info—a small magic trick inside the headline main stunt) while he's in charge, narrating the ninety-two pages, which, of course, he could not do, but we're going to let him anyway, with seemingly random swings of memory. We'll let our handicapped narrator just have at it, let him go where the wind takes him, using the typescript changes as a primary guide, but don't rely too much on that! Good. Keep reading. Oh—and that narrator section—let that be the opening section of the book. To get you in the swing of things.

Somewhere along the line, we learn that the family under examination (the Compsons) can claim a state governor and a general in the family tree; as well as an exotic expatriate forebear; an international conspirator and felon; and a first settler of the wilderness (and soon-to-be wheeler-dealer and Old South plantation baron). Fast forward to the present generation. The father is an intellectual, literary, despairing, idle, dying alcoholic; the mother an eternally whining, self-pitying, hypochondrial, guilt-and shame-dispensing nightmare; the oldest brother a suicide; the one sister promiscuous; another brother a sadist and small-town mercenary; the final brother mentally handicapped, the principal family shame, medically castrated by the preceding brother after an incident with a neighbor's daughter, then ultimately consigned to a state institution. All the children in one generation, one household. Did any editor suggest that this might be a tad much? One dementia too many? No? Well, while you're at it, throw in the sister's illegitimate daughter and one saintly, faithful African-American servant.

As a reading experiment, be a Southerner born in the twentieth century. For the fourth or fifth time, read the famous novel one week in April. Read it during Easter week, in a small north Louisiana river town, with the wisteria blooming just outside your window. A wall of wisteria, light blue and lavender, draped over the trees and fence rows, making tall oval mounds, curtains, over the pin oaks, along the bayou banks, like hovering ghosts. All of it blooming in the warm spring—a summoned horticultural cliché—wisteria, Lady Banksia rose, wild plum, crab apple, magnolia, azaleas, dogwoods, and vines and vines of honeysuckle. *Honeysuckle was the saddest odor of all*, Quentin, the mixed-up college kid, repeats over and over, in Boston in 1910.

In large part, it is only in the Appendix, written seventeen years after the novel, that the grand sweep becomes manifest—the author's signature romp through a familial, regional, global past—the novel as saga—with all the grandiose Faulknerian talk of time and land and striving and so on. The four hundred pages of the 1929 novel are actually a compact family soap opera. One entire section is almost exclusively a child's play. All those dinner-table disasters with Jason, Dilsey, the grandmother, and a sulking granddaughter. A scene echoed in a thousand television dramas and sit-coms.

Not surprisingly, you can spend a lifetime in the South and never once come across anyone who even remotely speaks like Quentin or his father Jason, or any character in this novel. True, in many small towns in the South, there are still one or two handicapped adult men accompanying their aging mothers to grocery stores. The usual liquor, drugs, and Bible Belt sexual explosions. Once proud plantation families still sell off old tracts of cotton land and soybean field, down to the last half acre, to be transformed into row after row of suburban lots and concrete driveways and backyard trampolines. But seldom those obsessions, that particular form of intensity. Your fault? Not traveling in fantastical enough, hyper-literate, alcoholic, near psychotic circles? Or a question of the nineteenth century? Or a question of rural, plantation Mississippi? Or, possibly, a question of the author as a self-contained universe?

Imagine the first-time reader, meeting the Benjy section right out of the gate, with its two Quentins, two Maurys, and a surprise name change to the main character. Often, two or three Jasons or Quentins or Maurys in the same sentence. Thirty-three-year-old Benjy hears a golfer cry out caddie (his sister, the novel's heroine is named Candace—shortened to Caddy) and dissolves into tears and moaning, then transmigrates to childhood. After a dozen or so readings, this is actually fun—identifying the stimulus/response cues whereby Benjy slips from thirty-three to five to eighteen.

In the Quentin section, the author weaves page after page of intricate, feverish, hyperbolic prose that defies you not just to guess what is happening, but when and where the action is taking place (or memory or conjecture or passion), and just who is doing the talking. And if you make a guess, then it plagues you with doubt that the speaker you finally settled on might actually have quit talking a page or so ago and this is his son or daughter or grandparent who is speaking now.

And don't forget that roster of Benjy-minders: Versh, T.P., Luster, and Dilsey's husband Roskus. But which of the minders are Dilsey's children? Which her grandchildren? The famous sasspril-luh-drunk scene. Drunk and mentally handicapped—there's a voice to impersonate! A wedding scene. Someone named Damuddy? Funerals galore. Fences, pastures, a branch. Dead Nancy (a mare). A universe of smells. Smells of leaves, of Caddy, of sleep, of trees. Dialect: I declare becomes "clare." As in "Clare if you don't put down that stick this moment!"

Occasionally, amid the swirling ghosts and nightmares and time shifts and convolutions, the reader is stunned by a quiet passage. During his walk outside Boston, Quentin meets two or three boys fishing the river. They inquire about his watch:

"'I broke it this morning.' I showed them my watch. They examined it gravely."

The reader's joy in "gravely" is like a small still moment during a hurricane. The reader undergoes a sort of odd remembrance that Faulkner is a writer after all—someone we pay money to in order to receive such little pleasures. We'd almost forgotten—seeing him for so many pages as a dervish, a soothsayer, a kind of incantatory dark angel.

Still, it's difficult to resist the all too obvious view of Quentin as self-parody: poetical Billy Falkner—impotent, frail, virginal, possessing a sensibility hypertrophied to the point of insanity. Quentin/Billy as the youthful artist and stylist quite out of control: *Dalton Ames, Dalton Ames, Dalton Ames!* He pushes, dares, the reader to give up entirely, to throw away one's marked-up text, charts, and timelines (some of us buy used blackboards at the school rummage sale to line our walls) with a groan of exasperation at the sheer verbiage of it all, at "lonely and inviolate sand"—then draws us back in at the last minute with some gesture—the lost Italian girl at the bakery, the boys at the river—some gesture of fineness and bewilderment and human loneliness.

The Jason section as comic relief.

The undisputed villain of the novel, Jason allows us to laugh (at last) primarily at him, at his apoplectic, unrelenting, impotent rage—all his schemes backfiring—this psychopathic sadist, this businessman, raging forever against the Jews, the blacks, the Yankees, his boss, his mother, his niece, Dilsey, Benjy, his dead brother, dead father, disinherited sister, mistress, the townspeople, show people, customers, farmers, rednecks, and Wall Streeters alike. Improbable that a stroke will not fell him by age forty. He's the one true comedian in the piece, our one chance finally to laugh, thank God, during the four hundred pages of more or less unrelieved tragedy and loss. Here he is, during a day spent chasing his niece all over town, finally spying on her in the woods:

> and then I happened to look around and I had my hand right on a bunch of poison oak. The only thing I couldn't understand was why it was just poison oak and not a snake or something.

He's an ordinary middle-aged, middle management, wage slave, slogging it out from paycheck to paycheck, with a dreary boss, dreary home life, everybody and everything to blame. He is wildly hilarious. And why not? An intolerable mother at home. A phenomenally vagrant teenage niece as a ward. Employees underfoot and undirectable. He is the sole financial support of an entire family plus servant hangers-on. (Although his income is augmented by thievery from Caddy.) A sadist, an irredeemable villain yes, but a perfect characterization of a million Americans—driven, beset, railing against government, the faraway rich, and local knavery.

A reader in these latter days, approaches this improbable novel with half a dozen chips on his or her shoulder. First of all, we don't even like Faulkner. The ridiculous syntax. The obsessions, oddities. All the lofty talk of honor, family, the past. Just as in the case of Yeats or Eliot, at other epochs, it is necessary to defeat him, get him out of your brainpan. Most Southern readers stay pointedly away, save for dipping into this one work every decade or so. This laughably impossible family. This ultra-literary stylization, utterly artificial and contrived, stepchild of Joyce's experiments.

Did Faulkner himself realize he'd better tone things down in Sections Three and Four, the Jason and Dilsey sections? Did he realize, during the writing, that he might not have a reader left standing after the Benjy and Quentin sections? Benjy thrown upon the unsuspecting American public in 1929 with only an obscure date as introduction. No epigraph, no chapter synopsis: *PART the FIRST, Where the Child Maury has his Name changed and goes on to watch His Sister climb a Tree.* No helpful reader's guide, no genealogy (he'd get around to that, somewhat, seventeen years later), no useful timeline, no colored inks (which he'd asked the publishers about!—paving the way seventy-five years later for Jonathan Safran Foer). Followed immediately by Quentin's meandering, self-annihilating dream. The sheer exhaustion of it all—psychic, emotional, mental—caused readers to abandon their books in despair, and the author must have foreseen this, decided to employ some straightforward narrative in the final two sections, which resemble, blessedly, the actions, speech, and descriptions of a workaday, sane writer. Although even here, he couldn't resist himself, creating the magnificent, irresistibly satanic Jason, through sheer voice, impersonation, malice, and humor.

By Section Four, pleased with this craftiness, he must have said, let's throw it all in—God, religion, the whole thing. And he pulls this off too. Mimics, impersonates, remembers, an entire coherent vocabulary of spirit and grace in the Easter Sunday passage, nine or ten incandescent pages out of the four hundred—the Reverend Shegog; the children frightened by Benjy; and Dilsey seeing the beginning and the end.

Section Four—the final movement—opens in a kind of unbearable silence and stillness. A device of the theater and symphony, which succeeds here deftly. One can almost see the stage grow dark, hear the murmuring in the seats, the coughing. The first three movements—Benjy, Quentin, Jason—have run their course; and according to the author in a famous attribution, there was nothing for it but to try once again: *The day dawned bleak and chill.*

In the end, worn out, furious at the wringer we've been put through, we still keep dumbly trying to puzzle out a specific object of loss that the author is so passionately relating. A woman? Love? Innocence? Doubtless true, but simultaneously not true, we guess. Nor the banal old Confederacy, obviously. Nor feudal clichés—plantations and steamboats; crinoline and cotton. In fact, these are barely mentioned at all. And surely not "Southern aristocracy," a comic phrase par excellence. (By the way, is any American aristocracy ever anything more than an homage and admission that some one of one's forebears was a more cunning, ruthless pirate than his peers?) But if not love, gold, cotton, the grand porticoed houses, then what? Why this furious congregation of words? Why *tear a passion to tatters*?

He hints at an answer in the Appendix, in a small passage when he names black-hearted Jason as:

> the childless bachelor in whom ended that long line of men who had had something in them of decency and pride even after they had begun to fail at the integrity, and the pride had become mostly vanity and self-pity . . .

Decency . . .

Characteristically, Faulkner no sooner gives us such a word than he snatches it back with "vanity and self pity." This kind of mordant authorial frankness and clarity is terrifying to behold, and we're glad such a gaze is not directed toward us. Still, perhaps that single word *decency* is what we get to hang onto after four hundred pages of a family's dissolution and grief. A quiet little word. Is it enough? *We have sold Benjy's pasture so that Quentin may go to Harvard* . . .

The brief passage continues. He names that long line of men, his Compsons—who had migrated from Scotland into North America into Mississippi—six generations of soldiers, gamblers, and dreamers. Finally down to the last generation, to the novel's current father—Quentin's and Caddy's and Jason's and Benjy's father—a cultured and literary drunkard "who sold the last of his patrimony not to buy drink but to give one of his descendants at least the best chance in life he could think of."

It's enough.

Portrait of the Spinster as a Young Woman

Elizabeth, thirteen, belongs to an affluent Nashville family. It is the turn of the century and she lives in a richly appointed mansion on Church Street, with a cook, an upstairs maid, and a houseboy to see to the needs of her father, her older brother, and herself. Lucy, the maid, has a bath ready at four, when Elizabeth comes home from the private school run by Miss Hood and Miss Herron.

There's a parlor downstairs that Elizabeth likes to sit in every evening while waiting for her father and brother to return from work and school—a parlor with a fireplace and a settee and a huge picture window, with mirrors she gazes into, like Alice with her looking-glass. Elizabeth tries to imagine what the future holds, letting her agile mind range over and parse and evaluate the events of the day, the events of her life, and the thousand other infinitesimal shadings, permutations, and gradations of meaning and emotion that adhere to and underscore every gesture made and every word spoken by her father and her brother and any other human being who happens to pass before her in the slow, somber, ghostly universe of this house on Church Street, where she is motherless, friendless, alone, terrified, waiting.

Elizabeth is the narrator and heroine of Peter Taylor's eerie, astonishing 1940 story, "A Spinster's Tale," Taylor's first major work, written when he was only twenty-one but already a Jamesian master of indirection and interiority.

Is Peter Taylor still read these days? Perhaps not. Perhaps the label of Southern man of letters, once considered a badge of distinction, has about it now the moldy air of a classroom, of chalk-dust and fatigue. And while it's true that Taylor's novels and stories are often set in the bygone era of Tennessee's high gentility (Vanderbilt University, servants, balustrades, and vestibules), we should no more overlook his fiction than we should dismiss *Dubliners* or the stories of Chekhov, also records of lost days.

Peter Taylor was born in 1917 in west Tennessee. He wrote three novels, eight collections of stories, plays, poetry. Received the Pulitzer Prize for his novel *A Summons to Memphis*. He died in 1994 at age seventy-seven.

Like Eudora Welty, another Southern writer who won't stay fixed in an assigned category, Taylor continually surprises—the ground shifts under us just when we think we have him safely pinned. In a story like "Two Pilgrims," Taylor's upper South intersects with a rural, poor-white, lower South: On an auto-trip from Memphis to Alabama, a middle-aged businessman and his best friend, a lawyer, spot a desolate farmhouse on fire, pull their car over, race into the house and begin rescuing the tawdry belongings of the farmer and his wife, who have never seen the two unexpected volunteers before and can only look on, amazed.

In "The Fancy Woman," Taylor takes us into the mind of a rich man's alcoholic mistress spending a week in the country. Josephine works at a third-rate department store, but we sense that her vocation is more nearly that of a kept woman, not far from a prostitute. Taylor takes us into her risky, wearisome, boozy, promiscuous world—of dinner parties with staring society ladies and half-grown sons who may or may not have "notions" of their own. In other stories, Taylor writes of an aged black woman at odds with the entire population of Thornton, Tennessee; of a weird brother-sister act in a disheveled mansion; of two college roommates in 1939 driving to New York City to meet their soon-to-be ex-girlfriends.

"A Spinster's Tale" is Elizabeth's autobiography, condensed to one year in her life, and then offered to us in the form of a horror story. Taylor gives Elizabeth an almost literal monster to fear—old Mr. Speed, a bedraggled, pathetic, incontinent alcoholic stumbling past her house two or three times a week, red-faced and cursing. Taylor takes us deep into Elizabeth's fright and obsession over Mr. Speed; our worst fear is that he might come up the walk one day and burst into the house to assault her—the door-crashing bogeyman of a thousand nightmares. Taylor tantalizes us with this possibility throughout the story—and then in the final scene, he brings it to pass. For a moment, here in this psychological study from a meticulous pathologist, we think we're on the verge of a slasher-film climax.

Elizabeth is named for her mother, who died after a stillbirth a few months before the main action of the story. Early on, Elizabeth describes the funeral for the infant when she accompanies her father and brother "to our lot in the gray cemetery to see the box (large for so tiny a parcel) lowered and covered with mud."

Parcel, of course, is a writer's word—in its wrenching, terrible perfection. Such language is a reminder that "A Spinster's Tale" is a reminiscence, narrated by Elizabeth as an adult. We almost overlook this. "A Spinster's Tale" is a classic framed short story, where the frames consist only of the words "when I was a little girl" in the first sentence and then the repetition of "little girl" in the final paragraph of the story. So who is speaking during the main narrative? Elizabeth at thirteen or the adult Elizabeth? The author would almost have us believe that it is the girl Elizabeth who is speaking, that her observations, self-descriptions, and verbal acuity are contemporaneous. Precocious child! Unlike, say, the trickster Nabokov, Taylor does not intrude his adult narrator into the middle of the story. Or perhaps the voices of the adult Elizabeth and the child Elizabeth are suspended together, beyond time, one and the same?

The deceased mother speaks only one line in the story, but it is spoken with deadly religious surety to Elizabeth's brother on a night the brother came home drunk, and remembered forever by Elizabeth: "Son, I'd rather see you in your grave."

And she means it. It is a Victorian mother's primal curse, spoken by a mother perhaps inconceivable to modern readers—violent, spiritual, victorious. She is already dead when the story begins and is never directly spoken of by husband, son, or daughter; yet, her words from the grave are a critical step in devising Elizabeth's despair.

At thirteen, Elizabeth is already evincing the first hints of the stress and near-paranoia that will eventually solidify into her adult madness—a functioning, manageable sane madness, which takes the form of perfect self-control and self-analysis and solitude and sufficiency. Of course, she is not alone. The brother and father also blithely enact their roles in Nashville's long-encrusted universe of puritanism, paternalism, and dementia.

One day, a crowd of the brother's friends comes to visit, inviting everyone to join them on a great outing, an automobile ride. Elizabeth remembers her father's response—a history of an era, in one line: "Father said, 'Sure. The more, the merrier.' But he declined to go himself and declined for me Henry's invitation."

Another occasion, Elizabeth remembers a rare moment of tenderness with her dying mother:

> I stood self-consciously straight, close by my mother, a maturing little girl awkward in my curls and long-waisted dress. My pale mother, in her silk bed jacket, with a smile leaned her cheek against the cheek of her daughter. Outside it was spring. The furnishings of the great blue room seemed to partake for that one moment of nature's life. And my mother's cheek was warm on mine. This I remembered when I sat before the gas logs trying to put Mr. Speed out of my mind; but that a few moments later my mother beckoned to the practical nurse and sent me suddenly from the room, my memory did not dwell upon. I remembered only the warmth of the cheek and the comfort of that other moment.

I stood self-consciously straight—to say the least! There is a longing and a solitude in these words almost too painful for us to read. *Against the cheek of her daughter.* Already objectifying herself, Elizabeth is estranged, alienated, near a breaking point. Then, a moment later, she sits with her brother and father in the parlor, listening to their customary chitchat—the memory of her mother now fading, her anguish over Mr. Speed foremost in her mind, superseding everything else in the daily challenge of living with two men in a cold house on Church Street: "I realized not that I was ready or unready for them but that there had been, within me, an attempt at a preparation for such readiness."

Then her imagination runs away from her: "But the conversation took insinuating and malicious twists this afternoon."

"A Spinster's Tale" is filled with these complex, fluted statements—the products of Elizabeth's rarefied articulation and of her barely maintained control. Like James Joyce's "The Dead," "A Spinster's Tale" is over-long and over-detailed, the kind of masterful indoors story that requires time and a slowly paced writing style to press into the further corners of domestic and psychic minutiae. Taylor taunts us with the seemingly sinister Mr. Speed, and then has us follow Elizabeth down the paneled hallways and gray rooms and long winter days of the house on Church Street—as we strain to decipher one convoluted, elliptical sentence after another, afraid for Elizabeth, afraid for everyone, afraid for ourselves. We can only watch as the faint presence, the warm cheek, of her mother is lost to Elizabeth, until it becomes a memory, a phantasm.

If the Blanche DuBois–type was one of the role models for nineteenth- and early twentieth-century Southern women in the contest between freedom and restraint, then Elizabeth represents another possibility: contained and frozen, given a respectable and useful social niche within Nashville's toxic gentility in return for her silence, her relinquishing of possibility, her solitude. The poet Philip Larkin could just as easily have been describing Nashville in "This Be the Verse" when he wrote of all those "fools in old-style hats and coats." Still we ask: Did Elizabeth herself take part in the working out of her future? Did she make choices along the way? We keep asking questions—but the author did not leave every answer in the story.

And yes, we get the point that Elizabeth is an example of submerged sexuality. It doesn't take a Freudian to tell us this. (Though if you want to, you can read "A Psychoanalytic Appreciation of Peter Taylor's 'A Spinster's Tale'" in the *Journal of Evolutionary Psychology*, 1988.) At thirteen, Elizabeth is both obsessed with, and horrified by, men, sex, herself. Closely observing her own long legs. Closely observing her long black hair ("heavy, dark curls hanging like fragments of hosepipe to my shoulders"). Everywhere she turns there are men and men's belongings, as if they left their scent-markings when they passed: Mr. Speed, her brother, her father, her two bachelor uncles, the Benton boys—all their masculine, loud, animated, disordered talk, their cars, machines, liquor, laughter, cigars, canes, the constant spitting, the brown stains of tobacco on white snow, the leather shaving straps . . . In her white nightgown, Elizabeth fantasizes that her brother is striking her. At one point, she actually invites him into her bedroom late at night, to sit on her bed; she throws her arms around his neck, weeps, smells his whiskey, and "his natural odor." She dreams every night, then diligently analyzes her dreams; in one she has huge hands and hides them "under her skirt." She teaches herself how to flirt with young Henry Benton: "In answer to his smile I said, 'Games are *so* much fun.'" She puts up her hair like an adult woman, prowls dark corners of the house, and, experimenting with her growing powers, succeeds in getting the cook fired. At the same time, she's still unable to control her paralyzing fears: fears of Mr. Speed, of drunkenness, and of men—men going to war, men at the train station, hundreds of them, so "close together."

Couldn't there have been one other sympathetic or sane woman on Church Street to befriend Elizabeth? A wise older aunt, a cousin? She doesn't even have any playmates, so far as we can see. No dog, no cat, no bicycle, no friend. She doesn't go into her own backyard, doesn't take a walk, or kick a ball. Wasn't there a single schoolmate's birthday party for her to attend that whole year? She's thirteen-years-old!

In the end, if "A Spinster's Tale" is nothing more than a case study, we can read it once and leave it, but the story's complex and overwhelming grief doesn't let us off easily. Instead, in 1940, Peter Taylor gave American readers one more installment in our long education in the craft of learning how to read. *Parcel.* At story's close, Elizabeth is safe in another house somewhere in Nashville, we assume. She is thirty, forty, fifty, we don't know. Doubtless, her father is long dead. Her brother gone, too, probably dead, perhaps a despairing glamorous suicide like Quentin Compson, or maybe just an ordinary drunk in Memphis or New Orleans. Elizabeth's mother has faded deeper into silence—lost along with everyone—husband, son, daughter. And then we remember that the mother was herself a recipient of pathology from the past. What was *her* childhood like? we groan . . . Larkin, again: *Man hands on misery to man.*

We try to imagine Elizabeth at the end of it all. The fine neighborhoods of Nashville endure. The Church Street house was sold years ago, no doubt. Elizabeth makes tea, recalls a few term papers that need grading, walks by a small window in her modest living room, and looks out.

Best Southern Short Story with a Drowned Bride, Alligators, a Fish Fry, some Light S&M, French Cinema, the Pearl River, Mel Gibson, and a Chicken

W*illiam Wallace Jamieson* . . . Just learning the hero's name in Eudora Welty's comic love-story-and-boys-adventure, "The Wide Net," a reader knows right away that here is another installment in the improbable, ongoing history of all those half-literate, half-mad Scotch-Gaelic emigrants who settled the wide swath of American forest, hill, and farmland from the Carolinas to Texas that we call the South. First published in *Harper's Magazine* in 1942, "The Wide Net" is the second funniest short story Welty wrote—after "Why I Live at the P.O.," its companion piece and literary opposite. Whereas "Why I Live at the P.O." is a domestic farce—a housebound monologue of woe—"The Wide Net" is a sun-drenched fairy tale, a Huck Finn river-journey, and a wise, tender depiction of marriage and young love.

Was romantic love an essential subject for the famously never-married Welty? If you're not sure, take a look at Tom Harris, the magnetic, handsome salesman in her short story, "The Hitch-Hikers," who seems to have a girl friend (or to have left a broken heart) in every whistle-stop in the Delta. Or the wary, circling couple in the mysterious "No Place for You, My Love." Rare among her stories, "The Wide Net" was given a dedication—to John Frasier Robinson—who, we learn from Welty's biographers, was one of her two great unrequited loves. The other was Kenneth Millar, a.k.a. the mystery novelist Ross MacDonald, an unobtainable, long-married Californian. In Robinson's case, homosexuality, rather than geography or a prior claim, was the obstacle to his role as Welty's leading man.

Robinson was a Mississippian, a writer, editor, man of letters, a combat veteran in World War II, and world traveler—who, over the course of their long friendship, told Welty dozens of stories of his growing up in the Delta, one of which provided the kernel for "The Wide Net." (His great-grandmother's diary inspired Welty's novel *Delta Wedding.*)

And for anyone wondering how a soft-spoken, infinitely well-mannered Southern woman like Welty knew so much about fishing trips and careering bands of tatterdemalion boys running wild in the woods, just remember that Welty was the older sister of two brothers, all three of them growing up in the half-rural South at the turn of the century. A writer of Welty's imaginative powers wouldn't need but a single summer with two such brothers to bankroll a lifetime's worth of male characters. The aging, spectral "Miss Eudora," attended by acolytes from Millsaps College, was only one of the roles this freelance writer played in her long, shaggy, bright, and irregular American life.

Although nine-tenths of "The Wide Net" concerns a crowd of boys spending a day on the Pearl River, the center of the story is the young farm couple, William Wallace and his strong-willed wife Hazel (they seem to be about seventeen or eighteen years old). Hazel is three months pregnant when we meet her, and lately subject to odd moods and humors. Callow, mystified William Wallace on their farm near the tiny village of Dover doesn't have any experience with pregnant wives (no Oprah or Dr. Phil in 1940s Mississippi);

and, in a country boy's mild rebellion, he takes off on an all-night drinking spree, ends up sleeping in a ditch, and finally rolls home about daybreak to find Hazel gone and a note explaining that she has drowned herself in the Pearl River. Welty sketches all this in the story's opening paragraph:

> William Wallace Jamieson's wife Hazel was going to have a baby. But this was October, and it was six months away, and she acted exactly as though it would be tomorrow. When he came in the room she would not speak to him, but would look as straight at nothing as she could, with her eyes glowing. If he only touched her she stuck out her tongue or ran around the table.

Four brief sentences—and we can already see and comprehend a bewildered young Mississippi husband, as well as make out the rough outline of a spirited young teenage wife. Hazel is given little physical description by Welty—other than "golden-haired" and pretty: "the prettiest girl in Mississippi." She hardly appears in the story (she speaks only a few lines at the beginning and end), and yet her presence outweighs Welty's large, noisy cast of scruffy male characters. She's a lithe girl-woman who possesses the kind of headstrong feistiness and rural brio that has been flummoxing the William Wallace Jamiesons of the South for two hundred years.

Early in the story, William Wallace recalls the day he first courted Hazel (she was walking home from her grandmother's house with a dinner-bound live chicken under her arm):

> I says, "Where are you taking the fryer?" and she says, "Mind your manners," and I kept on till after while she says, "If you want to walk me home, take littler steps."

Alone, chicken in hand—and she's able to apprise herself of a social situation in two seconds. Able to identify a young man as a suitor, size him up, give him the green light to commence courtship, and also let him know who's in charge—all in a moment's time, in mid-stride along a Mississippi dirt road, and all with a perfectly maintained straight face. *Take littler steps . . .*

Naturally, Hazel isn't dead. This is probably the worst kept plot secret in short-story history. Everyone knows that she will reappear at story's end: the reader, William Wallace, his best friend Virgil Thomas, as well as the raucous band they enlist to drag the Pearl River—the Malone brothers, the Doyle brothers, Old Doc (owner of the wide net and a chattering dispenser of rural wisdom), plus two pairs of little-boy brothers, one black, one white. Twenty-one searchers in all. Their excursion to the Pearl River takes up the bulk of Welty's long story; their ramble is a rollicking mock-epic and quest.

Welty shapes the day on the river as a series of wonders—a sequence of carefully wrought scenes—cinematic, leisurely, deftly paced:

> They went on and suddenly the woods opened upon light, and they had reached the river. Everyone stopped, but Doc talked on ahead as though nothing had happened. "Only today," he said, "today, in October sun, it's all gold—sky and tree and water. Everything just before it changes looks to be made of gold."

The Pearl River is Shakespeare's forest of Arden, of course. The boys have left home and village for the express purpose of seeking magic—sky and tree and water made gold. (Besides Shakespeare, one also thinks of Turgenev and his burnt-golden rural scenes in *A Sportsman's Sketches*.) All day long, the list of wonders grows. At first, the wide net gathers up armfuls of catfish which the boys save in buckets. (The Malones and Doyles have come along mostly for the fishing.) Fat eels slip uncaptured through the seine. The bottom of the river, they're surprised to find, is littered with cast-off shoes. Once, someone cries a warning and everyone moves aside to let four or five alligators swim by. (They capture a baby alligator for a pet.) Then they raise a bedraggled human river-rat from his sandbar hideout. While they break for lunch on the bank, another river-dragon swims by: It is the "King of Snakes!" they all cry—a kind of Mississippi Loch Ness Monster.

Someone must have brought matches, for they fry up a meal of the catfish and stuff themselves and then fall asleep on the sandbar like rustics in a Winslow Homer painting. A great thunderstorm arrives while they linger ashore. Welty, an adroit cinematographer, lays on extravagance after extravagance:

> A huge tail seemed to lash through the air and the river broke in a wound of silver. In silence the party crouched and stooped beside the trunk of the great tree, which in the push of the storm rose full of a fragrance and unyielding weight.

The cleansing storm marks the end of the river-dragging, the end of the quest. No one's wife has been retrieved by the wide net—alive or drowned—but by this time hardly anyone remembers why they came to the woods in the first place. No one except William Wallace, who has maintained a kind of alert, astonished fury throughout the day. Maybe 5 percent of his brain believes that Hazel might have actually jumped in the river. In any event, the rite of river-dragging is a punishment he knows he must endure, and, in the most memorable image of the story, he dives and dives to the bottom of the river, searching for his lost love in the water's depths.

Curiously, this scene is almost an exact replaying of the 1934 French film, *L'Atalante*, another tale of a young married couple's strains. In *L'Atalante*, the French bridegroom Jean has been told that you can see the face of your beloved by looking into any vessel of water. When his young bride runs away from him, Jean, a barge captain, dives overboard into the Seine and plunges as deep as he can. There in the murk, the image of his beautiful wife appears before him, arrayed in bridal white, floating, just out of reach. (Is there a chance that the cosmopolitan and well-traveled Welty might have seen this film?)

As the late afternoon skies clear, the boys and men straggle into town. William Wallace returns to his farmhouse and observes one last wonder. Above his roof—a rainbow at night! Naturally, as soon as he steps inside, Hazel calls out his name. She's been there all the time:

> After a moment, he smiled, as if no matter what he might have hoped for in his wildest heart, it was better than that to hear his name called out in the house. The voice came out of the bedroom.
>
> "What do you want?" he yelled, standing stock-still.
>
> Then she opened the bedroom door with the old complaining creak, and there she stood. She was not changed a bit.
>
> "How do you feel?" he said.
>
> "I feel pretty good. Not too good," Hazel said, looking mysterious.
>
> "I cut my foot," said William Wallace, taking his shoe off so she could see the blood.
>
> "How in the world did you do that?" she cried, with a step back.
>
> "Dragging the river. But it don't hurt any longer."
>
> "You ought to have been more careful," she said.

After supper, the two sit outdoors for a while on the front steps. William Wallace asks Hazel where she had been that morning. When she says that she was hiding under the table only a few feet away while he read her note, he gives her a soft tap and slap, then turns her over on his knee and briefly, amorously spanks her. *Angrily* and amorously, we gather. This is only a tiny moment in the story but its most erotic moment—a kind of tender, absurdly charming poem to married love:

> "Do you think you will do it again?" he asked.
>
> "I'll tell my mother on you for this!"
>
> "Will you do it again?"
>
> "No!" she cried.
>
> "Then pick yourself up off my knee."

> It was just as if he had chased her and captured her again. She lay smiling in the crook of his arm. It was the same as any other chase in the end.
>
> "I will do it again if I get ready," she said. "Next time will be different, too."

Next time . . . Excellent parting shot. And those two exactly-placed exclamation points! The story ends with Hazel leading William Wallace into the house, taking him by the hand, "smiling as if she were smiling down on him." Her young husband has spent a day in an enchanted forest, but if he lives to be a hundred, he will find no wonder or marvel in the state of Mississippi or anywhere that surpasses the mystery of his beautiful wife leading him to bed.

How Far into Grief, Disaster, or Horror?

Violet Karl, the narrator of Doris Betts's 1969 short story, "The Ugliest Pilgrim," is twenty-eight-years-old and lives alone on a mountain near Spruce Pine, North Carolina. Her father died five years ago; her mother died when she was a child. Her hair is dingy; she has a wide nose, pimpled chin, small breasts. All in all, she's a scrawny, homely mess; and worse, she has a scar on her face curving like a bright ribbon from nose to ear. Strangers turn their faces when they meet her.

But today is May 29, 1969, and Violet is taking the Greyhound to Tulsa, Oklahoma, to meet a TV evangelist named the Preacher and be transfigured into someone beautiful—or, at least, into something better. In fact, any improvement at all will do, and Violet's willing to bargain if it comes to it.

Soon into Betts's picaresque American road story, the reader has only one question: What form will Violet's disappointment take? Just how far into grief, disaster, or horror is the author planning to lead us? Betts, who was born in 1932, is a North Carolina native and professor emerita at UNC. Her writing career got off to an early start when she won a *Mademoiselle* short-story contest as an undergraduate, then published her first collection of stories around the same time, in 1954. She worked for a number of years in the newspaper business before settling into her long university career, publishing six novels, three short-story collections, essays, and criticism, and gathering a trunkful of fellowships and awards along the way. Among her works, the widely anthologized "The Ugliest Pilgrim" is perhaps her best known. (In a kind of literary trifecta, it has also been made both into a short film and a musical, winning an Academy Award and a New York Drama Critics Circle Award respectively.)

Early in "The Ugliest Pilgrim," Violet reveals that she keeps an envelope full of Bible citations to help her pitch her case to God and the Preacher—whichever is in the giving vein. She's a wary, untutored mountain girl, who, other than her father, has never had a close friend, and on first meeting her, we expect another one of those Flannery O'Connor grotesques that overpopulate Southern literature. But Violet isn't just another hillbilly zealot. She's also a careful Bible researcher, an alert traveler, a shrewd observer of others, and a self-deprecating memoirist. Nor does she mind taking a drink now and then (she started at fifteen with her father). She's a good poker player (father again), and though her love life is thus far nonexistent (she's had only one brief, unmemorable sexual experience in her life, a high school boy on a dare), Violet is one of American fiction's great romantic heroines—irresistible, witty, desirous.

The story begins as a comic miniature:

> I sit in the bus station, nipping chocolate peel off a Mounds candy bar with my teeth, then pasting the coconut filling to the roof of my mouth. The lump will dissolve there slowly and seep into me the way dew seeps into flowers.
>
> I like to separate flavors that way. Always I lick the salt off cracker tops before taking my first bite.
>
> Somebody sees me with my suitcase, paper sack, and a ticket in my lap. "You going someplace, Violet?"
>
> Stupid. People in Spruce Pine are dumb and, since I look dumb, say dumb things to me. I turn up my face

> as if to count those dead flies piled under the light bulb. He walks away—a fat man, could be anybody. I stick out my tongue at his back; the candy oozes down. If I could stop swallowing, it would drip into my lung and I could breathe vanilla.

Breathe vanilla . . . Short story readers tend to be diehard voluptuaries, always searching for two separate aspects of a piece of fiction: the lyric and the tale. Like readers of thrillers or mysteries, we're as addicted as the next guy to the joy of turning pages, joy of the ripping yarn. But before that, we are mesmerized by sentences, phrases, the sounds of words. The occupational hazard is that we will get stuck in some convoluted James Joyce or John Cheever paragraph unable to get out. *The way dew seeps into flowers* . . .

The hazard for Doris Betts in a faux-naïf story like "The Ugliest Pilgrim" is that her dizzying impersonation of Violet might eventually tip over the edge and become precious or simply virtuosic. It doesn't. It is Violet herself, through wit and intelligence, who prevents the story from capsizing. On the bus, when she is asked, "And you live by yourself?" she instantly thinks, "No, there's men falling all over each other going in and out my door." Violet has lived in solitude for so long that she has developed the bemusement and irony and acute powers of observation of a literary loner, a stranger in a strange land, a pilgrim.

Although Violet is a lively believer in God's promises, she admits to a touch of skepticism towards the likes of the Preacher (a stand-in for Oral Roberts, it seems); what's more, somewhere along the way, she's been given immunity from American Christianity's chronic sexual repressiveness. Maybe it was her childhood, running wild in the mountains with nothing but deer and screech owls as companions. Whatever the case, she's as sexually exuberant as a barn cat, and able to have a one-night stand with a soldier in a fleabag Memphis hotel and then praise God for the opportunity. In Violet, author Betts has given both Sunday School teachers and country parsons a bewildering character study and a wicked stumbling block to routine moral preaching.

During Violet's love scene with her newfound soldier friend Monty, she says, "He feels his way onto the bed and he touches my knee and it changes. Stops being just my old knee, under his fingers. I feel the joint heat up and bubble . . ."

Violet is speaking in full elliptical style. *He touches my knee and it changes* . . . We are almost in Faulkner's Benjy voice, the faux-naïf of all faux-naïfs: "Caddy smelled like leaves and like when she says we were asleep."

She continues:

> One time he stops. He's surprised, I guess, finding he isn't the first. How can I tell him how bad that was? How long ago? The night when the twelfth grade was over and one of them climbed with me all the way home? And he asked. And I thought, *I'm entitled.* Won him a five-dollar bet. Didn't do nothing for me.
>
> But this time I sing out and Monty says, "Shh," in my ear.

Monty is a blue-eyed paratrooper that Violet meets on the bus. He and another soldier Flick, who is black, play poker with Violet, tell her stories, take her out to eat and to a movie. But we tremble when they invite her to spend the night with them in Memphis. (Lord, is this the tragedy Betts is leading us to?) Wisely, Violet is given a room of her own with the two men down the hall. They are ordinary raw young men, certainly on the prowl, as ready as the next soldier for a sad pick-up like Violet, but in the midst of drinking and carousing, the two men surprise themselves. Their story is one of learning to *see* Violet. Without quite knowing how it happens, they watch as she becomes a complex being who cannot be dismissed out of hand. Given the chance, Flick wouldn't mind sleeping with her, but as the hours pass, he recognizes that Violet and Monty are pairing off as a couple. By story's end, he's content to be a third wheel. Monty is crude, ignorant, self-engrossed, repelled by Violet's looks, and no doubt he comes to her room in the night with little more than a young man's curiosity and opportunism. But he too is transformed. Bit by bit, the two men turn out to be decent.

The next day, the journey continues. The night with Monty was bliss, but Violet hasn't come this far to miss Tulsa and the hoped-for healing. Monty and Flick get off the bus in Fort Smith, Arkansas: a sad parting, with promises to meet again. Monty is a dream for sure, but the change Violet seeks in Tulsa demands her. And what if it is only pity Monty offers? Violet recoils from the possibility. Her mind swirls with a dozen conflicts, but on that point she is adamant. She'll give him up before settling for pity. In fact, she doesn't plan to look for him in Fort Smith on the trip back. If she sees him, she'll run.

Oklahoma is a treeless, baking wasteland—the green forests of North Carolina a lifetime away—and Tulsa itself is a metallic, noisy hell of cars and crowds. Violet takes a room in another lonely hotel room. After she makes her way to the "Hope of Glory Building," she discovers that the Preacher is out-of-town: He records his "shows" ahead of time. Violet is shuffled from one office to another, finally pawned off to a young assistant minister, who predictably advises her to accept God's will, to understand that beauty is transitory. Shaken, she offers him her envelope of scriptural passages. Their debate is straight out of the Book of Job. When the young assistant piously instructs Violet, "We must all trust His will," Violet magnificently replies:

> After all these years, isn't it God's turn to trust mine? Could He not risk a little beauty on me? Just when I'm ready to ask, the sober assistant recites, "'Favor is deceitful and beauty is vain.' That's in Proverbs."
>
> And I cry, "'The crooked shall be made straight!' Isaiah said that!"

The next day—with no sign of a miracle—Violet is back on the Greyhound for the long trip home to Spruce Pine. By now, the reader is numb, wondering with what painful twist Betts is going to contrive Violet's ultimate loss—the theme of every great short story, from "The Overcoat" to "The Dead" to "Guests of the Nation" to "Bartleby the Scrivener." Once again, she's seated on a dismal bus seat, her head slumped against "the white rag they button on these seats." We're approaching Fort Smith, where we left Monty and Flick. Tulsa and the Preacher, wearisome frauds, are behind us.

Of the hundred and fifty prayers in the Book of Psalms, a handful are known as the "imprecatory" or hard psalms—containing curses, malice, bloodshed, and the psalmist's sincerest hope and prayer that God will smite dead the next ten thousand Amalekites who show up looking for a fight—make their women barren, dash their babies on rocks, etc.

Fiction writers tend to be inspired by this same dark muse. Once in a while, though, they relent from their steady diet of mayhem, grief, and tragedy, and offer us a variation on the writer's art. So it is with Betts and "The Ugliest Pilgrim," in which she utilizes a little of everything: a first-person narrator; a love scene; a dream sequence; theology; topical satire; wild comedy; and finally, a surprise ending (which, of course, you are encouraged to experience yourself) that transforms this story from a predictably hard psalm into an unexpected psalm of praise.

Quartered

Mention the phrase "New Orleans writer" to a native of the city, and the names offered in nomination will come back at you fast. Whom did you leave out? One of the olden greats, like George Washington Cable or Lafcadio Hearn. Or a contemporary—from the list of fine writers that seems to grow by the season: Ellen Gilchrist, Richard Ford, John Biguenet, Tom Piazza, Nancy Lemann, Patty Friedmann, Moira Crone . . . put seven names on a list and ten have been left off.

Then there's another list, from the period between the very old and the contemporary: Walker Percy, Elizabeth Spencer, Hamilton Basso . . . whether from Mississippi, from northern Louisiana, or maybe as a transplanted native, everyone seems to have at least one New Orleans story in them.

Some outsiders can't get enough of the city. Drawn there by some half-baked dream of drinking absinthe in Pirate's Alley or, if they've got any sense, by the saner dream of eating oyster po-boys and sloshing down beers during the winter season (maybe also for part of the spring; okay, through May at the latest, before the heat arrives in its dementia-inducing omnipresence).

Even O. Henry wrote a New Orleans story—"Cherchez la Femme," complete with a surprise ending, a pleasantly screwball plot, and a "little, Creole-haunted café of Madame Tibault in Dumaine Street." We get to meet a pair of jocular newspaper reporters, the Little Sisters of Samaria, and a mysterious Mr. Gaspard Morin, recently deceased, who may or may not have misappropriated twenty thousand dollars from Madame Tibault . . . and on and on.

But whom should readers turn to when looking for an authentic New Orleans literary voice? Anne Rice?

The Big Three show no signs of falling in the polls: *A Streetcar Named Desire*, *A Confederacy of Dunces*, and *The Moviegoer.* Is this a good thing? Like three massive oak trees in Audubon Park, they risk blocking sunlight from getting through to smaller plants.

Tennessee Williams has his own annual tourist convention, complete with Brando-wannabes braying, "Stellllla-a-!" in the French Quarter, and out-of-town academics hosting discussions on the wit and wisdom of Blanche DuBois. ("Please don't get up," Blanche liked to say, while passing the four bestial card players for the fortieth time.)

A life-size bronze of Ignatius J. Reilly now stands on Canal Street at the site of the old D.H. Holmes department store. Do pilgrims come and make their obeisance to sardonic, long-winded old Iggy? Do they touch his statue, like rubbing the worn toe of St. Peter in Rome? What would Ignatius think of his teary-eyed fans? Would he offer them a Paradise Vendors hot dog—albeit a bit dusty and tattered—from his coat pocket?

And after Walker Percy gave us William Holden strolling down Royal Street in the opening chapter of *The Moviegoer*—one of the best scenes Percy ever wrote—with the morose Northern boy on his honeymoon finding redemption by lighting Holden's cigarette in such a perfectly casual gesture, man to man . . . and the flummoxed ladies from Hattiesburg . . . and the philosopher, Binx Bolling, tagging along behind them all, taking in the sights, observing, sizing things up according to Kierkegaardian categories—well, what New Orleans writer wants to compete with that?

What are the small fry to do?

At first glance, New Orleans seems to be the perfect locale for a writer—physically circumscribed between the river and the lake. Intensely exotic, almost extra-planetary, with its own vocabulary; its own botany (like a North American Galapagos); its own intricately-layered social, ethnic, and racial hierarchies.

And, by now, we know the famous names by heart (we've taken the walking tour), all those writers who passed through the city, spending a season or two in the French Quarter, while doing graduate work in belles-lettres and whiskey: Faulkner, Williams, Capote, Sherwood Anderson, Zora Neale Hurston, Kate Chopin . . .

The question is: where is the great New Orleans novel? Yes, John Kennedy Toole gave us Ignatius, comedian-saint for the ages. The sheer bliss of listening to Ignatius chat with his mother about employment prospects:

> "I doubt very seriously whether anyone will hire me."
>
> "What do you mean, babe? You a fine boy with a good education."
>
> "Employers sense in me a denial of their values."

Yet *A Confederacy of Dunces* comes up short as a coherent work of fiction—it is overwritten, floundering, all over the map. And Walker Percy wrote *The Moviegoer* in his early Camusian, European existentialist phase—in it, he deftly offers a few choice tidbits of city locution: Mrs. Schexnaydre, Gentilly, Faubourg Marigny. But for those of us already charmed by the bright musings of Binx

Bolling—well, we would have read the novel with the same close attention if Percy had set it in Birmingham or Santa Fe.

It has often been suggested that New Orleans itself is the reason for this failing. The place is just too rich, too exotic, too delicious for its own good. All those lyrically-ringing street names and wine-viney locations—Jackson Square, Tchoupitoulas Street, the Garden District, Canal Street. Walker Percy knew he had to get out of the city (had to hide out in Covington) if he wanted to continue as a writer; otherwise, he might have wound up as just another local colorist or architecture expert or garrulous habitué of the Quarter.

How odd that America's most cosmopolitan city has produced so little indisputably great fiction in its three hundred years of existence, while a forgettable, dried-up little college town in north Mississippi could produce in one brief burst (the spring of 1928) a single work (*The Sound and the Fury*), that, cavalierly and almost insolently, over-shadows the combined literary oeuvre of the city's glamorous cast of novelists and story-writers.

The term "a writer's writer" implies limitations. It's like calling someone "a fine stylist," or "an under-rated author."

But it's difficult not to apply the term to Shirley Ann Grau. Born in the city in 1929, Grau won the Pulitzer Prize in 1965 for her novel, *The Keepers of the House*, and is the author of five other novels and three collections of short stories. Her work has appeared in *The New Yorker*, *The Atlantic Monthly*, *The Southern Review*, *Cosmopolitan*, *Mademoiselle*, etc. She received the 2004 Louisiana Writer Award; holds two honorary doctorates; yet whenever I bring her name up in conversation with reading friends, I always get the same answer: "Know the name; haven't ever read her."

In interviews, she has made it quite clear that she doesn't like being labeled a Southern writer. I'm certain that Grau wouldn't approve of being called a "New Orleans' writer" either. Indeed, her fictional settings range from New Orleans to the East Coast, to Chicago, to Europe, to South Africa. She writes in women's voices, men's voices, black or white voices, of every age and background.

Still, *The House on Coliseum Street* (1961), her second novel, is about as close to a pure New Orleans novel as you can get. It is the story of Joan Mitchell, twenty-years-old, living with her mother and half-sister in upper class 1950s New Orleans—an era of long-entrenched dating rituals and courtship rites. When Joan turns up pregnant, her mother speeds her off to the Gulf Coast for an abortion and a discreet vacation with relatives. Joan's urbane, nominally Catholic mother (she has been married five times) is blithely nonchalant when speaking with her daughters about sex, marriage, and men. Provincial readers might find themselves a bit shocked to meet such a debonair and witty family in supposedly ultra-bland 1950s America. Grau writes of them in an unblinking, unhurried, clean-lined American prose. Here, she is describing Coliseum Street, its quiet rhythms interrupted by a drifter wandering in from the river slums several blocks away:

> The street closed up on itself, like a doodlebug rolling into a ball. The houseboy who had been hosing down the front walk at the Forstalls left his hose, pausing only to turn off the water, and disappeared around the back. The Edwards' maid, a tall skinny black woman who had spent most of the morning sweeping and cleaning the front porch so that she could see who was entertaining for lunch, flicked back into the door with only a switch of her yellow uniform. A nurse came and got the Villere girl who was playing in her swing in the side yard of the corner house. She yanked her out of the swing without a word and carried her off screaming and kicking.

A few chapters later, describing another characteristic New Orleans scene, Grau reveals herself to be a specialist in the blasé surprise, dropping a quiet death or two among the camphor trees and sweet olives:

> September was ending in its usual way, with sharp gusts of wind and grey sheets of rain. On the porches, leaves were jammed through screens like vegetables through a sieve. There were the usual hurricanes in the Gulf, hurricanes heading for the Texas coast. Once one passed so close that the gigantic neon clock advertising Jax beer (on lower St. Charles Avenue) got ripped off like a top-heavy flower. Coming down, it squashed two or three people, happy drunks who had come out of a nearby bar and were watching to see it fall.

Hurricanes, death, flowers—in lesser hands, items like these are the stuff of Southern cliché. But Grau's literary powers are such that her lushly-described New Orleans never tips over the edge, never becomes a parody or a camp grotesque like the ludicrously overgrown gardens and psyches in *Suddenly Last Summer.* By the end of *The House on Coliseum Street*, young Joan Mitchell has survived her year-of-living-dangerously, but barely—for a time she turns herself into a stalker and wreaks vengeance on her former boyfriend, by getting him fired from his job and chasing off his new girl. She outmaneuvers both her kid sister and her mother, and gains ascendancy of Coliseum Street—Joan will inherit the house one day—but we're not sure how long she will stay in New Orleans.

Older than Grau by twenty years, Eudora Welty gave her fictional Mississippi rustics a holiday in 1952 and offered us her own take on New Orleans via the mysterious story, "No Place for You, My Love."

This is a kind of love story in reverse, a sideways love story—it is Welty at her most elliptical, compacted, and nearly impenetrable. A pair of Northerners meet as strangers at Galatoires one Sunday afternoon. The man is long-married, quietly cynical, available for an affair, it seems, but not much more. The woman, as far as he (and we) can tell, is in love with another man—alone for the moment, working out some knotty love-problem of her own. These two wary, circling, non-lovers decide to take a spin below New Orleans. "South of New Orleans? I didn't know there was any south to *here*," the woman says as they depart.

For these two strangers, New Orleans fulfills its stock role as an exotic foreign land, but they soon discover a deeper, unimagined exoticism in their long car trip into the bayous and swamps. Here is a sublunary, malarial terrain, of fishermen, and ferry rides, oyster shells, crawfish scuttling across the highway, and a roadhouse café in Venice, Louisiana, the last stop before you fall off the end of the world:

> Below New Orleans there was a raging of insects from both sides of the concrete highway, not quite together, like the playing of separated marching bands. The river and the levee were still on her side, waste and jungle and some occasional settlements on his—poor houses. Families bigger than housefuls thronged the yards. His nodding, driving head would veer from side to side, looking and almost lowering. As time passed and the distance from New Orleans grew, girls ever darker and younger were disposing themselves over the porches and the porch steps, with jet-black hair pulled high, and ragged palm-leaf fans rising and falling like rafts of butterflies. The children running forth were nearly always naked ones.

The further south they drive, the stranger the geography, and the dreamier their own mental states. (Shirley Ann Grau takes us into this same riverine otherworld in her story, "Joshua," about a black fisherman settlement in a nearby locale.) The couple (who are strangers we have to keep reminding ourselves) are thrown together for nearly seven or eight hours in their long drive south then back north to New Orleans, and Welty has them speak only a handful of lines of dialogue. The result is that Welty has written the mood story of all mood stories, hyper-saturated with imagery, densely and joyously descriptive—on a metal-decked ferry, crossing the Mississippi with the sun crashing down, the woman thinks, "It was like riding a stove."

Welty's story is a river journey into a half-benign, half-terrifying heart of darkness. But nothing happens. The couple stop for an hour or so in the roadhouse in Venice, dance together to a raucous jukebox, observe the poker players, drunks, children, bartenders, and denizens of this waterworld. On the drive back, they kiss—once, briefly, knowing that nothing will come of it.

At story's end, in the midst of the travelers' grogginess and fatigue, Welty plays a small joke on us, by letting New Orleans become a place of safety and stability, a welcome and hoped-for sanctuary:

> Over the levee wall now, like an aurora borealis, the sky of New Orleans, across the river, was flickering gently. This time they crossed by bridge, high above everything, merging into a long light-stream of cars turned cityward.

The lights of the city are lying before them, guiding them home.

Truman Capote was no outsider. Although he grew up in Alabama and New York, Capote was born in New Orleans and never tired of calling himself a native of the city.

Abandonment was his theme in story after story, novel after novel. He told abandonment stories in the lonely-childhood tale, "A Christmas Memory," and then again, somewhat obliquely, in *Breakfast at Tiffany's*, as well as in *Other Voices, Other Rooms*, plus a number of the short stories, even in *In Cold Blood*—there, by way of the ghastly, blood-soaked Perry Smith, who was a kind of negative of an artist, forever lost and searching, on some two-lane highway, at least during the periods he wasn't locked up in jail.

Had Capote been alive in August 2005—what would he have thought when his hometown—an entire city!—found itself abandoned by a country which had never been too sure it really belonged in the USA in the first place? Such a peculiar city, New Orleans, everyone said—half foreign, half insane, and a welcoming host to every kind of wickedness. Maybe it didn't deserve saving? Would he have laughed or wept?

When he was twenty-one, Capote spent a few months in an apartment in the Quarter—the obligatory writer's sojourn in New Orleans, close on the heels of Faulkner and Williams. One of the results of his brief visit was an essay for *Harper's Bazaar* (1946), later collected as "New Orleans" in his *Selected Writings*.

The essay is a memoir-impressionist piece—a small hodgepodge really, plus sketches of two or three local Quarter types—capturing in a handful of pages what many novels fail to do in five hundred:

> New Orleans streets have long, lonesome perspectives; in empty hours their atmosphere is like Chirico, and things innocent, ordinarily (a face behind the slanted light of shutters, nuns moving in the distance, a fat dark arm lolling lopsidedly out some window, a lonely black boy squatting in an alley, blowing soap bubbles and watching sadly as they rise to burst), acquire qualities of violence.

If he'd cared to, Capote could easily have been another Joseph Mitchell, ferreting out saloons and fish houses from New Orleans to New York, and telling us their stories as Mitchell does in *Up in the Old Hotel*. Capote again:

> The torn lips of golden-haired girls leer luridly on faded leaning house fronts: Drink Dr. Nutt, Dr. Pepper, NEHI, Grapeade, 7 Up, Koke, Coca-Cola. N.O., like every Southern town, is a city of soft-drink signs; the streets of forlorn neighborhoods are paved with Coca-Cola caps, and after rain, they glint in the dust like lost dimes. Posters peel away, lie mangled until storm wind blows them along the street, like desert sage—and there are those who think them beautiful; there are those who paper their walls with Dr. Nutt and Dr. Pepper, with

Coca-Cola beauties who, smiling above tenement beds,
are night guardians and saints of the morning.

Surely, Ignatius Reilly would have been pleased to see his favorite soft drink here—Dr. Nutt.

When reading New Orleans literature, one should always end with a music story. In "Talk to the Music," Arna Bontemps writes a comic coming-of-age story of a young African-American man at the turn of the century. Norman Taylor is around eighteen or nineteen, and has arrived in the city from Rapides Parish with the intention of enrolling in "New Orleans University." At least that is what his parents believe, but Norman is mad about music, mad about the blues, mad especially about the blues singer Mayme Dupree—whom he describes as the precursor of Ma Rainey and Bessie Smith, as well as the inspiration for Jelly Roll Morton and Sidney Bechet.

Bontemps (1902-1973) was born in Alexandria, Louisiana, and grew up in California. In the 1920s, he made his way to New York, published poems as a member of the Harlem Renaissance, later moved about the country, eventually becoming head librarian at Fisk University in Nashville. Editor, poet, novelist, historian, scholar, he taught in New York, Chicago, and Alabama, and published dozens of books, including many anthologies of African-American literature in collaboration with Langston Hughes.

Bontemps's young hero, Norman, in "Talk to the Music" finally tracks down Mayme Dupree—she's playing nightly gigs in a Storyville brothel. Norman has already created a vision of a blues singer in his mind—an artist living in pain, suffering for her art; part saint, part mystic, part martyr: "I was curious about the woman herself and couldn't stop wondering what it was that troubled her and made her sing the way she did."

Mayme gives Norman a sideways dismissive glance, but lets him speak with her, lets him hang around her a few weeks, like an underfoot but harmless child. Her own description of her artistry has little in common with Norman's romanticism:

> Along about nine or ten o'clock I sit down at the piano, and I sets my bottle of gin where I can reach it. I don't stop playing and singing till that bottle's empty. Then I get up and put on my hat. They pay me my money and I go home.

But Norman, the young scholar, persists. He gains entry to the Storyville brothel and hears Mayme play in person. As everyone else in attendance, he is moved nearly to tears by her performance—surely here is the secret heart of the blues. Riding home with Mayme, he tries to explain her to herself, lecturing her on rhythms, themes, angels and innocence.

Bontemps ends "Talk to the Music" with a perfect throw-away line, a classic freeze-frame. Mayme is speaking to poor Norman, but she might as well be speaking to all of us—who are outsiders coming to New Orleans, literary tourists trying to puzzle out the secrets of the city, confident that we can get to the truth if we study hard enough:

> She pondered this conceit as the hack jogged homeward in the early dawn, and I thought it was making a good impression until she suddenly said, "You're crazy."

The Piano Player

Fiction writers are usually canny enough not to tackle music as a subject. I'm speaking here not of "musical prose" or "poetic prose," which any mediocre novelist can churn out, but of the attempt to evoke an experience of music through words. E.M. Forster's Beethoven passage in *Howards End*, along with Tolstoy's "The Kreutzer Sonata" are commonly named among the successes in the field. Most writers of the genre make one or two looping circles around some "musical moment," describing a few feelings and impressions. But does anyone really get to the heart of it?

Consider the South's holy trinity of letters—Faulkner, Welty, O'Connor. There's hardly a music story in the bunch, other than Welty's extraordinary, jazz-inspired "Powerhouse," the exception that proves the rule.

My favorite music story before Welty is Ivan Turgenev's short story "The Singers" (first published in 1850) from *A Sportsman's Sketches*. The narrator of this collection is an aristocrat who wanders the redneck steppes of Russia with only a dog, a gun, and an occasional rustic sidekick. In his blasé, leisurely rambling, he brings to mind two or three generations of hunting-obsessed Ole Miss lawyers and planters' sons in their khakis and artfully mud-daubed boots.

Still, unlike his dubious New South descendants, Turgenev's nobleman maintains a sense of humor, and manages to travel great distances with modest means (little more than a knapsack, really, spending uncomplaining nights in whatever barn or chicken coop he's offered). In "The Singers," he stumbles into the village of Kolotovka, an outpost of stupefying bleakness—two or three shacks in a burned-out landscape. Its citizens are amiable enough, however, and we soon learn that a singing contest is about to take place between the local favorite, Yashka the Turk, and a rival named "the booth-keeper from Zhizdry." The scene is the local tavern. The winner gets a pot of beer, and everyone in town is already three-quarters drunk.

Turgenev plays an old writer's trick on us in "The Singers," one known as the "feint and jab." (It's a variation on the surprise ending, part of every writer's toolkit of tricks and pranks.) In this case, the stunt consists in letting the challenger sing first—and appear to win outright with a deeply moving performance. Much patting on the back, congratulations, "old fellow, surely you've won," etc.

Then it's Yashka the Turk's turn, the local favorite (he's called Yakov). The English translation of Turgenev's nineteenth-century prose is as purple as Faulkner's, unashamed of its high emotions:

> He gave a deep sigh, and began to sing . . . The first sound of his voice was faint and unequal, and seemed not to come from his chest, but to be wafted from somewhere afar off, as though it had floated by chance into the room . . . The first note was followed by another, bolder and prolonged, but still obviously quivering, like a harpstring when suddenly struck by a stray finger it throbs in a last, swiftly-dying tremble.

> He sang, utterly forgetful of his rival and all of us; he seemed supported, as a bold swimmer by the waves, by our silent passionate sympathy. He sang, and in every sound of his voice one seemed to feel something dear and akin to us, something of breadth and space, as

> though the familiar steppes were unfolding before our eyes and stretching away into endless distance. I felt the tears gathering in my bosom and rising to my eyes.

Yakov wins! He ends his song in rapture and ecstasy with everyone in the tavern sobbing and blubbering in his beer, with wet embraces and promises of eternal camaraderie. Even the boothkeeper from Zhizdry concedes defeat with dignity.

Almost a century after "The Singers" (and a universe apart), Eudora Welty decided to give music writing a whirl in her exuberant, complicated 1941 story "Powerhouse." She wrote it after hearing Fats Waller one night in Jackson, Mississippi. She said that she went home after the concert and composed the story in a single draft (much like the all-nighter that resulted in her landmark story "Where Is the Voice Coming From?" about the murder of Medgar Evers), writing in a raffish style that she had never attempted before (and never attempted afterward). There were no revisions, no deletions or changes. She woke up the next morning, took a look at her pages, and, as if awakening from a kind of working trance that led to a story so far outside her normal range, decided to simply let it breathe.

Today, when reading "Powerhouse," we can almost imagine the author's intoxication that night in a small room in her house in Jackson—words and exclamation points flying, Fats Waller's adrenaline-fueled improvisations becoming her own, and Welty racing hard to get all the words down. An astonishing authorial feat: unleashing a torrential flow of inspired prose and editing herself simultaneously. This kind of virtuosity is akin to the split-in-two brains of the very dance-band musicians she was describing. (In her opening passage she describes them from the point of view of the white audience at the segregated concert—the racist mentality of 1940s Mississippi.) Powerhouse's band members are urban black jazzmen in a backwater Southern town, putting on their standard show, able to roll through the familiar list of songs and audience requests—the same tunes night after night, town after town—and simultaneously able to let loose their energy, communicating with one another, it seems, telepathically, with absolutely no idea how any particular set of variations is going to be shaped, going to end.

The story should probably always be read aloud, at night, to a noisy crowd, with a door at the end of the hall that someone keeps opening so that the lights from passing cars sweep across the room. Among this story's many pleasures are:

Nine songs: These are actual songs from the 1920s and '30s, by various composers and lyricists—the titles of which are sprinkled throughout the story. Together they make a kind of nine-line American poem:

> Marie, the Dawn Is Breaking
> Honeysuckle Rose
> Pagan Love Song
> Empty Bed Blues
> Tuxedo Junction
> Sent for You Yesterday
>   and Here You Come Today
> The Goona Goo
> San
> Somebody Loves Me

A shy, pretty waitress: She works in a woebegone café in a black neighborhood, serving Powerhouse and his entourage during intermission of the concert and dance. She is awestruck, joyful, terrified, and fearless, and in only five or six lines of dialogue, nearly walks off with the story:

> "Never seen you before anywhere." The waitress moves and comes forward and slowly shows little gold leaves and tendrils over her teeth. She shoves up her shoulders and breasts. "How I going to know who you

> might be? Robbers? Coming in out of the black of night right at midnight, setting down so big at my table?"

Powerhouse himself: New York-born Fats Waller (1904-1943) played stride piano, wrote jazz, big-band tunes, popular hits ("Ain't Misbehavin'"), and wrote Broadway shows; appeared in films, toured Europe, toured the U.S., lived the prodigious, anarchic life we expect of music legends, and died in a Pullman car of pneumonia and accumulated psychic and bodily disasters. But beyond any Waller model or inspiration, Powerhouse is sufficient unto himself—pianist, singer, bandleader, Dionysian, dervish, poet, and king. Welty keeps him in motion almost every moment, feet slamming the piano pedals, manic fingers on the keys, head, lips, voice, everything "going all the time, like skating around the skating rink or rowing a boat." In the midst of the fray, she notes that, "He listens as much as he performs . . ." and later, "He loves the way they all play, too—all those next to him." A towering mad artist—and a collaborator? Welty has piled on the contradictions intentionally. She wants us to break under the strain.

Film Noir: The story doesn't have any plot to speak of. Like Fats Waller, Powerhouse provides a running commentary during his performances, speaks over his own lyrics, ad-libs, talks more or less all the time—to the band, to the audience, to the air, to himself. His band members are a team of virtuosos, capable of answering the boss's questions in the middle of a set, then bantering casually among themselves. In the midst of one song, Powerhouse tells them he just received a telegram. His wife, Gypsy, is dead, has jumped out of a hotel window in grief and despair. We readers have no idea what to make of this. Is this a real event or part of the song the band is playing? A spoof of some long-lost ballad? Is he really married? Who is Gypsy? The inner circle of band members (Valentine, Little Brother, and Scoot) reply calmly to Powerhouse's announcement. It's not until later, in the café that we realize that Powerhouse is creating a fiction, improvising, inhabiting a genre as familiar to his band as train schedules or weather reports. He's telling an old, old story, a musician's cliché—a lonely wife in a hotel room, suspicion, jealousy, death. Here is Gypsy in her nightgown one minute, then blood and gore on the sidewalk the next. Then, he creates a magical, form-changing comic villain named Uranus Knockwood (along the lines of Humbert Humbert's nemesis Clare Quilty), author of the terrible message—the telegram message, which eventually becomes a refrain: Your wife is dead. Your wife is dead. Hangers-on in the café listen, bewildered. The story is tossed from one band member to the next, growing, taking on enhancements, everything getting wilder and wilder. Eventually, the hangers-on, the band, all of us, find ourselves in on the joke. (Although the beautiful waitress is still not sure: "All that the truth?") The tragedy, blood and death, grief and destruction, are so outrageous, so clearly a fiction, that finally everyone can laugh—in a desperate relief, a release.

Sharply timed comic dialogue: Like this take on Uranus Knockwood, the stealer of other men's wives—the band members batting their lines back and forth like three or four Estragons and Vladimirs on a desolate Mississippi stage set:

> "Why, he picks her up and carries her off!" he says.
> "Ya! Ha!"
> "Carries her *back* around the corner . . ."
> "Oh, Powerhouse!"
> "You know him."
> "Uranus Knockwood!"
> "Yeahhh!"
> "He takes our wives when we gone!"
> "He come in when we goes out!"
> "Uh-huh!"
> "He go out when we comes in!"
> "Yeahhh!"
> "He standing behind the door!"
> "Old Uranus Knockwood."
> "You know him."

"Middle-size man."
"Wears a hat."
"That's him."

One superb Welty line: "A screen door warped like a sea shell."

The band: Starting a new song, tuned, fierce, alert:

> "You-all ready? You-all ready to do some serious walking?"—waits—then, STAMP. Quiet. STAMP, for the second time. This is absolute. Then a set of rhythmic kicks against the floor to communicate the tempo. Then, O Lord! say the distended eyes from beyond the boundary of the trumpets, Hello and good-bye, and they are all down the first note like a waterfall.

Who can deny that Welty's music-writing experiment gives Turgenev's "Singers" a run for the money? (A year later, in 1942, she even wrote her own Turgenev story, "The Wide Net," a comic boys' adventure on the Pearl River.) Did she do it, though? Achieve the impossible—capture an experience of music in fiction? Welty would probably admit that she failed here, too—the gap unbridgeable, but a memorable failure.

For such a plotless story, Welty decided to end it with a song: "Somebody Loves Me" (lyrics, DeSylva and MacDonald; music, Gershwin). A member of the audience has requested the famous tune, and the band dutifully plays it, chorus after chorus: *Somebody loves me, I wonder who!* Over and over, Powerhouse sings the familiar verses, asking a single question: I wonder who? I wonder who?

Welty answers him in an eerie, joyous last line.

Frank O'Connor

In 1918, a fifteen-year-old boy from an impoverished family in County Cork, Ireland, joined the Irish Republican Army. Michael O'Donovan served in the IRA's First Cork Brigade during the period of turmoil and violence that followed the Easter Rising of 1916. O'Donovan continued as a Republican who fought against the National Forces loyal to the Irish Free State during the Civil War of 1922-23, eventually being taken prisoner and serving time in an internment camp.

Then, in 1931, the same Michael O'Donovan, now a twenty-eight-year-old writer with the pen name Frank O'Connor, published a short story called "Guests of the Nation," which remains today, seventy-eight years after it was written, a masterpiece of the short story form.

The plot is simple. Sometime in the 1920s, two low-ranking English soldiers have been captured by the IRA as a reprisal after the similar capture of some Irish soldiers. The two English hostages are then shuttled about the countryside from one farmhouse to another, while reports filter in from Battalion headquarters. The question no one wants to face is: What will happen if the English execute the prisoners that they are holding? What will the Irish do with their own two prisoners, their "guests"?

The English soldiers—tall impassive Belcher and the short, nonstop-talker 'Awkins—are ordinary Army time-servers, who've had the bad luck to be posted to Ireland during the current Troubles, and the even worse luck to have been captured by the IRA. (Which, for these two, was not too difficult a feat, one imagines.)

Their life as prisoners, however, is not that bad. They play cards every night with their two tenders, Noble and Bonaparte; and they gab all day long with whatever aged widow or grandmother they happen to be lodged with. Always a farmhouse in the middle of nowhere. Always a grumbling old woman, puttering about and cooking supper for the four men. There's a fireplace to stretch your legs against. There's pious Noble (his brother is a priest) whom 'Awkins can argue with about religion, capitalism, politics, what-you-will. Bit by bit, captors and prisoners become friends—"chums" as the taciturn, shambling Belcher puts it.

The young Irishman Bonaparte narrates the story, and, at least at the beginning, looks upon his charges with a wry amusement, bored with his own superiors at being given such a dubious assignment:

> I couldn't at the time see the point of me and Noble being with Belcher and 'Awkins at all, for it was and is my fixed belief you could have planted that pair in any untended spot from this to Claregalway and they'd have stayed put and flourished like a native weed.

Eventually, an IRA officer named Jeremiah Donovan arrives from headquarters with the news Bonaparte and Noble are dreading: The English have executed four of their prisoners. What will happen now? Bonaparte wants to know. What will happen to Belcher and 'Awkins?

O'Connor traces out the last moments of the story in an unflinching terrible irony—in which everything is centered on the word "duty." Donovan, a self-assured Battalion man, announces his task with a stern, barely muted excitement. He is only following orders, he insists, doing his duty, enacting justice. "There were four of our lads went west this morning," he says, "one of them a boy of sixteen."

Now, we readers can only look on, while O'Connor leads us alongside the men, on the short trek into the bog. We watch poor 'Awkins as he grovels and begs for his life:

> "Listen to me, Noble," he said. "You and me are chums. You won't come over to my side, so I'll come over to your side. Is that fair? Just you give me a rifle and I'll go with you wherever you want."

O'Connor's prose is neither sensational nor moralizing, yet he spares us nothing:

> I alone of the crowd saw Donovan raise his Webley to the back of 'Awkins's neck, and as he did so I shut my eyes and tried to say a prayer. 'Awkins had begun to say something else when Donovan let fly, and, as I opened my eyes at the bang, I saw him stagger at the knees and lie out flat at Noble's feet, slowly, and as quiet as a child, with the lantern light falling sadly upon his lean legs and bright farmer's boots. We all stood very still for a while watching him settle out in the last agony.

A few moments later, they shoot Belcher. Then they bury the two of them where they lie, there in the bogland.

The fictional events described in "Guests of the Nation" are, by now, nearly a hundred years old. Yet the story's vocabulary seems as familiar to us as the vocabulary of our present day news—prisoners, reprisals, claims to justice—words soaked in blood, words that are still being offered to us by today's executioners, only in new guises, new languages. "You understand it's not so much our doing. It's our duty, so to speak," Jeremiah Donovan tells Belcher, just before raising his pistol.

At the end of "Guests of the Nation," after Noble and Bonaparte return from the bog and put their shovels and things away, they are met by the fierce old woman of the house who asks them again and again of the Englishmen, "What did ye do with them?" She already knows the answer.

In the last paragraph of the story (one of the most beautiful and moving passages in any literature), the narrator Bonaparte cannot bear to face the old woman. He realizes that he is a prisoner himself forever:

> So then, by God, she fell on her two knees by the door, and began telling her beads, and after a minute or two Noble went on his knees by the fireplace, so I pushed my way out past her, and stood at the door, watching the stars and listening to the damned shrieking of the birds. It is so strange what you feel at such moments, and not to be written afterwards. Noble says he felt he seen everything ten times as big, perceiving nothing around him but the little patch of black bog with the two Englishmen stiffening into it; but with me it was the other way, as though the patch of bog where the two Englishmen were was a thousand miles away from me, and even Noble mumbling just behind me and the old woman and the birds and the bloody stars were all far away, and I was somehow very small and very lonely. And anything that ever happened me after I never felt the same about again.

After publishing "Guests of the Nation" in 1931 when he was only twenty-eight, Frank O'Connor went on to become an eminent twentieth century author—playwright, novelist, short story writer, critic, poet, and translator. He died in 1966 at age sixty-three. For myself, "Guests of the Nation" holds first place among all of O'Connor's works. This story of revenge and violence—Belcher, 'Awkins, Noble, Bonaparte, the farmhouse deep in the country, the dark Irish night. "Guests of the Nation" is a terrifying story to read, yet our experience of O'Connor's artistry transfigures our despair into a tiny particle of hope.

Isaac Bashevis Singer's Perfect Short Story

How often is the title of a short story memorable or even necessary? You are halfway through a piece in *The New Yorker* and suddenly find yourself flipping pages backwards, asking, "Now *what* is this thing called?" In rare cases (like Hemingway's "The Short Happy Life of Francis Macomber"), a title can actually perform a role in the plot. Mostly though, titles are summary notions, names of characters or places, ironic tokens, occasionally a one-line poem. Coming upon Isaac B. Singer's "The Cabalist of East Broadway" (from the collection, *A Crown of Feathers*, 1973), a reader's first response is anxiety—not the best way to begin reading a short story. What is all this business of the Cabala, of mysticism? Are we to be stymied at the outset, we wonder, due to our ignorance of *The Tree of Life*, *The Angel Raziel*, and the world of emanations? A distressing way to start.

In any event, Singer's first sentence quickly calms our fears: "As happens so often in New York, the neighborhood changed." From this quiet opening, Singer flows into a long description of New York—inventing lower Manhattan both in a present 1970s and a remembered '30s and '40s. He has us eat lunch in a cafeteria; introduces his hero, Joel Yabloner; touches on the Cabala—all seemingly routine exposition—yet, the reader wants to live inside Singer's paragraph, wants never to leave that cafeteria, the smell of coffee, the nonstop talk. All of which is set in motion by Singer's modest first sentence and the word "changed"—a word which contains the whole story.

Singer is writing in his New York voice here—his narrator, the familiar nameless alter ego of himself, born in Poland, a writer of Yiddish stories, often about ghosts, sprites, dybbuks. This impersonation of himself, this Polish émigré, is one of the most appealing voices in American fiction. (But how, we ask, can such language, such lucid and hilarious American prose, be a *translation*?)

"The Cabalist of East Broadway" is composed of three sections, separated by a passage of years, separated by oceans—New York, Israel, New York. Cafeteria, banquet, cafeteria. It is a story of improbable meetings, lost chances, transitions, duplications, reduplications, and lists. At times, we fear that the author is going to stumble while balancing all of these ingredients (he doesn't):

> One could meet Yiddish writers, journalists, teachers, fund raisers for Israel, and the like.
>
> Blintzes, borscht, kreplech, chopped liver, rice pudding, and egg cookies.
>
> His apartment on Broome Street had no bath, telephone, central heating.
>
> I took part in the banquet—ate the nuts, almonds, avocados, cheese, bananas that were served.

Early on, while Singer is cruising through his opening exposition, he introduces his hero with the sly sentence: "Each time I entered the cafeteria, I would immediately see a man I'll call Joel Yabloner." Yabloner is a solitary, wizened, half-dead, impoverished old scholar. So far so good, but why the "I'll call"? Why this old-fashioned writer's artifice? We've already suspended disbelief—we gave him that, the moment we opened the book.

Later in the same section, Singer offhandedly mentions a certain "Eiserman, the dentist who had translated Shakespeare's sonnets into Yiddish"—an off-the-wall aside worthy of Gogol. And immediately after this nonsense about the dentist, he begins a dialogue with Eiserman himself, while the narrator is seated in the exam chair! An impossible and audacious transition which we hardly even notice.

All of this trickery is a sidelong lead-up to the introduction of Deborah Soltis, Yabloner's long-lost love from his youth. Joel and Deborah were two shy scholars, reading books together, never kissing. They were chaste lovebirds whose entire *histoire d'amour* consisted in looking up words in "Ben-Yahudah's great dictionary" and discussing "the fine points of grammar." Singer's brief sketch of their innocent and improbable love story is a comic miniature.

For the story's first major section break, Singer employs another one of his quiet, seemingly simple sentences: "Eventually, I stopped going down to East Broadway." By now, the reader is so hypnotized by the author's subtle style and enormous wit and humor that such a little sentence is delicious in itself. He pulls "eventually" out of his bag of tricks, and we know we are being tricked and we simply smile and nod and ask for more.

Then we learn that the forgotten, aged Yabloner has mysteriously appeared in Israel—in paradise—now cared for by followers, giving lectures, newly married, healthy, fit, secure. In a superb sentence, the narrator says, "The Jewish state has resuscitated Joel Yabloner." We are halfway through a three-thousand-word short story and the unexpected appears in the plot like something out of a thousand-page novel. Years have passed; the author has shifted scenes across oceans, breaking every rule of the genre; and we don't murmur a single objection.

One thinks of O. Henry, Maupassant, Saki, etc. and wonders if the surprise ending is intrinsic to the short story or is passé. Singer has employed a surprise middle here.

Later, our narrator happens to visit Israel, and in a traveler's coincidence, he stumbles upon Yabloner in a crowded hotel, giving a lecture to fervent admirers. After a banquet, he has a word with the reborn Yabloner and asks why he had stayed so long in America, alone and neglected, while paradise had been here in Israel all along. Laconic Joel shrugs and replies: "Man does not live according to reason." A characteristic Singer line, utterly simple in rhetoric, yet the reader sighs with pleasure. It is one of those lines that rises out of a story and settles in the reader's permanent memory like Melville's "I would prefer not to" or Joyce's "Snow was general all over Ireland."

Part Three opens with another deadpan sentence: "Again a few years passed." What can we do but shout with joy at such recklessness? Singer has established such blasé control over his material that he can play with us at will, and it occurs to us that perhaps "The Cabalist of East Broadway" consists of nothing more than the author's suavely disingenuous transitions: *again; someone told me; in connection with this* . . . and most outlandish of all, at the very end of the story: "Another idea came into my head."

Eventually, the narrator has business back in the old neighborhood in New York and drops by the cafeteria for coffee. Singer gives us a reprise of the opening paragraph—an old Jewish neighborhood nearly vanished, except for "some synagogues, yeshivas, and Hasidic study houses that had refused to leave." Wonderful to refuse . . .

And Joel Yabloner is back in America!

Alone and destitute, just as at the beginning. After a surprise middle, Singer gives us a surprise ending. Change upon change upon change. At no point has the story delved into the Cabala or into esoteric studies, but has itself become a mystery. Stunned, the narrator can only ask himself questions. Then, he tells us: "A few weeks later, I read among the obituaries that Joel Yabloner had died . . ." In this last paragraph, the narrator asks six questions in a row, thereby breaking any remaining writing rules he hasn't already broken. But what more could the poor man do? Layer upon layer of mysteries have unhinged him.

Singer chose a classic repetition ending for the last line of his story. In such an ending, the writer retrieves an image or line from some unobtrusive previous part of the story and repeats it as a final punch line. This new version illuminates the first and is in turn illuminated itself, in being seen twice. At its highest form, the repetition ending sets up rapid-fire light shows that emanate throughout the whole story, like a pinball machine hitting every bell and light. All writers use this ending at some time. Robert Frost used a compressed, surreal version in "Stopping By Woods on a Snowy Evening."

Singer chose *not* to use any of the other classic short story endings: the symphonic ("The Dead"); the freeze-frame ("Araby"); the lyrical ("The Country Husband"); the lyrical-dramatic ("Guests of the Nation"); or the surprise ("The Open Window"). Looking closer, we notice that he has used a rare double repetition—whereby *two* items are summoned from earlier in the story (Deborah Soltis and "Man does not live according to reason.") As we read and reread these last words of the story, we are nearly delirious, considering the permutations, the doubling and redoubling. We are as dazed as Singer's narrator. What is left for us but question after question?

Home for the Holidays

By now, most of the details of Truman Capote's lonely, cinematic, and barely-plausible childhood are well-known. Born in 1924 in New Orleans, he was a de facto orphan by age one or two. His disastrously mismatched parents had married in 1923, when the bride was seventeen, the groom twenty-five. Lillie Mae Faulk was a petite country beauty who wanted out of the dried-up town of Monroeville, Alabama. Archulus Persons, Jr. (called Arch—his name, like hers, sounds made-up) was another Southern cliché, a fast-talking, would-be entrepreneur and get-rich-quick artist, but mostly a freeloader and con man. In the biography *Capote*, author Gerald Clarke lets us follow the young couple's early life: Arch ran out of money on their honeymoon and sent his bride back to Monroeville to the very same wearisome, crowded house that she had been so desperate to escape—over-filled with Lillie Mae's aging Victorian cousins—three spinster sisters and a bachelor brother. Arriving in town a few weeks later, Arch was summarily tossed out on his ear. When he managed to talk his way back into everyone's good graces, he joined Lillie Mae in her old room, quite happy to live in the same house with his teenage wife's relations.

Arch Persons belongs to that great line of catastrophic, charming, and self-pitying American dreamers and frauds that stretches from the duke and king in *Huckleberry Finn* through Maury Bascomb in *The Sound and the Fury* down to almost any present-day late-night telemarketer or Bible-waving politico caught in a prostitution sting. He sold bookings on Mississippi River steamboats, managed a boxer, produced vaudeville/midway acts—the Great Pasha, the "World's Foremost Man of Mystery." Clarke lists other schemes: "a plan to syndicate shorthand lessons in newspapers, a magazine for sororities and fraternities, a series of popularity contests for high school girls." Arch schemed, finagled, went broke again and again, barely stayed two steps ahead of the law, sometimes not even that.

When Lillie Mae found herself pregnant at eighteen, she immediately made plans for an abortion—she was living apart from Arch, taking business courses in Selma—but she couldn't arrange things by herself in rural Alabama. Arch stalled and stalled in his promises to help her, but apparently he secretly wanted an heir, and thus Truman Persons (he would take his future stepfather's surname at age ten) was born in 1924, in Touro Infirmary—the expectant mother having been sent to New Orleans by the Monroeville cousins to receive better care than Alabama had to offer.

The marriage was over—probably ever since that truncated honeymoon—even though a divorce wouldn't be final until 1931. In Clarke's biography, we don't receive a blow-by-blow timeline, but during those eight years, the couple drifted to and fro, sometimes living together, more often not. And, in the meantime, Lillie Mae's latest avocation—apparently a kind of payback and gift to herself for being forced into motherhood—was a six-or-seven-year experiment in epic promiscuity.

For a middle-class girl born into turn-of-the-century rural Alabama, Lillie Mae took to the decadent life with an avidity worthy of our own digital-age crowd of girls-gone-wild. According to Clarke, the multi-cuckolded Arch even kept a tally of her adventures: twenty-nine at one count—college boys, foreigners, small-town studs, what-have-you. Arch wasn't beyond trying to parlay Lillie Mae's catholic and prolific screwing into profit: perhaps her lovers could help him kite checks or open a few business doors. He thought he'd hit the big time when heavyweight champ Jack Dempsey picked her up in a Pullman car for a brief, motorized coupling. Arch managed to enlist Dempsey as referee in a wrestling match he was promoting in Mississippi, but a rainstorm cancelled the show and Arch lost money once again.

As the marriage spiraled to its sorry end, Lillie Mae finally escaped from Alabama and made it to New York. There, she found herself a businessman named Joe Capote, changed her name to Nina, and reinvented herself as a Park Avenue wife. She died in 1954 at age forty-nine of alcohol and drugs, just as her son would do thirty years later.

But during the early days when Arch and Lillie Mae were still married, young Truman was carted around the country like an inconvenient pet and dropped off with relatives according to whatever whim struck the improbable couple. Occasionally, he was left with Arch's mother in Florida; most of the time with Lillie Mae's relatives in Monroeville, north of Mobile. Some of the periods when he lived with his parents, they devised a cheap babysitting service by locking him in a hotel room and leaving him there while they were out on the town. The child would scream unceasingly until he couldn't scream anymore and fell silent in exhaustion.

As if that weren't enough, the future author was often forgotten, assumed to be asleep, in the same room where Lillie Mae was having sex with one of her swains—the boy deposited on a nearby sofa or maybe in the same motorcar. Clarke records more than one such scene—in some anonymous lover's nest, even in his grandmother's house. By age four, Truman was a regular visitor to the Monroeville family house; by age six, he was a full-time resident.

From 1930 until 1932, Truman lived in Alabama in the custody of his four distant cousins. These are the famous Monroeville years; years of his literary formation—Portrait of the Artist as An Even More Peculiar Little Boy than You Might Have Expected—with Harper Lee as a childhood playmate; his parents' marriage sputtering through its last months; and a sixty-year-old cousin, Sook, one of the three spinster sisters, offering him probably the closest thing to love and affection he'd ever known. In a household of eccentrics, Sook held first chair: she was more or less homebound, pathologically shy, considered "simple" by outsiders, was cook, cleaning lady, babysitter, also herbalist, morphine-user and Bible-reader, who had never seen a movie and had barely traveled beyond the county line. In photographs of the period she looks seventy-years-old, close to eighty.

For Capote fans, Sook is the obvious inspiration for the 1956 short story "A Christmas Memory," a perennial holiday favorite (a standard on the dinner-theater circuit and on public radio readings, as well as the source for two television specials) about a young boy's lonely Alabama childhood with an aged female cousin. The two of them, the seven-year-old narrator and the sixty-something spinster, are both orphans and castoffs grudgingly given bed and board by unloving Christian relations.

Is "A Christmas Memory" a retelling of Capote's childhood recuperated in the form of a short story?

Well, yes and no. Sometimes readers forget about that traditional writer's habit of lying with almost every breath. And the fiction-writer's essential craft—transmogrifying people and places into the new reality of art—well, that's also a bit tricky to understand, even for the writers themselves, who are usually better off not thinking about the process, simply doing it. After "A Christmas Memory" was published in 1956, family members from Monroeville were known to complain that they weren't as poor or eccentric as Capote portrayed them. Towns-people also get confused when famous writers come home for a visit, eat dinner with the relatives, greet a few old friends: Honey, this is Truman; we were in third grade together. Having no idea in the world just how far gone the returning ones are now—the Faulkners and the Capotes and the Hemingways. Having no idea that the newly-famous one you are sipping tea with is a simulacrum, closer to a charlatan or an empty husk than the dimpled schoolmate you remember smiling in a photo album.

Fortunately for us, "A Christmas Memory" stands on its own and doesn't require an author's biography or a hermeneutics. The story, of course, is an elegy and a memoir of innocence—but one that rides so close to sentimentality and outright deadly sweetness that at times a reader sees the plot less in terms of character than in terms of the author's literary daring: Just how close to nausea and preciousness does he plan to take us? Will the whole thing capsize into an episode of *The Waltons* or a Hallmark Movie of the Week? Reading "A Christmas Memory" in 1956 might have been a more interesting exercise if one could have foreseen the day nine years later in 1965, when Capote dropped the following non-Hallmark moment into *The New Yorker* readership's mild and decorous living rooms—an oft-quoted passage, probably his most famous:

> Just before I taped him, Mr. Clutter asked me—and these were his last words—wanted to know how his wife was, if she was all right, and I said she was fine, she was ready to go to sleep, and I told him it wasn't long till morning, and how in the morning somebody would find them, and then all of it, me and Dick and all, would seem like something they dreamed. I wasn't kidding him. I didn't want to harm the man. I thought he was a very nice gentleman. Soft-spoken. I thought so right up to the moment I cut his throat.

So much for *The Waltons*. How, then, does "A Christmas Memory" get away with it? Its golden glow of memory, its needy little boy and the eccentric spinster; its cold fall morning which announces the onset of the Christmas season as fruitcake weather? The opening paragraph is enough to suggest that a moist eye might not be far away:

> Imagine a morning in late November. A coming of winter morning more than twenty years ago. Consider the kitchen of a spreading old house in a country town. A great black stove is its main feature; but there is also a big round table and a fireplace with two rocking chairs placed in front of it. Just today the fireplace commenced its seasonal roar.

But take another look at that innocuous word: *Consider.* Could one say that the author is already distancing himself, however microscopically—pulling away from us, as coldly and surely as he would later (infamously—according to current theories) distance himself from dour Dick Hickock and that blood-stained ghastly dwarf, Perry Smith? And please note the fireplace which "commenced its seasonal roar." Memoirists in the South are legion, but they are usually not *writers*. Herein is the strange disconnect at the heart of "A Christmas Memory." We acknowledge that Capote is slumming, giving himself a holiday, playing to the Radio City crowd in all of us; and yet those first nine or ten paragraphs are near perfect prose—Capote's rhetoric as balanced, precise, and cleanly-sculpted as Hemingway's or Joyce's. It is as if he couldn't stop himself from being a tough-minded compositor—even when writing about homemade kites, dogs, and orphans.

The story contains one funny line. The narrator (called Buddy) and his aged friend (she doesn't have a name in the story, she is simply called "my friend") make up one of the most charming pairs of literary heroes in the Southern canon. Chronically broke, they hold rummage sales, sell blackberries and flowers, scrimp and save every dismal penny and dime they can find:

> To tell the truth, our only *really* profitable enterprise was the Fun and Freak Museum we conducted in a back-yard woodshed two summers ago. The Fun was a stereopticon with slide views of Washington and New York lent us by a relative who had been to those places (she was furious when she discovered why we'd borrowed it); the Freak was a three-legged biddy chicken hatched by one of our own hens. Everybody hereabouts wanted to see that biddy: we charged grownups a nickel, kids two cents. And took in a good twenty dollars before the museum shut down due to the decease of the main attraction.

A perfect word like *decease*, in its deadpan hilarity and sheer Joycean surprise, is almost too good for its own sake, almost outweighs the rest of the story—the reader's ears stand instantly alert. No one in Monroeville ever struck a witticism like that.

In terms of plot, there's not much to the story—Capote fans know it by heart. Buddy and his friend make fruitcakes, make Christmas kites, are each others best friend. The older relatives dutifully enact their roles as evil step-cousins: Buddy is a captive prince held prisoner in the black castle. It is the last Christmas together for the seven-year-old boy and his friend; soon, the narrator will be sent away to military school. There are a few letters over the years; the friend grows older, less agile, dies.

As over-used as the phrase may be, there is still some truth to the well-worn "artist as monster" theme. They will consume anything—memories, family, neighbors, lovers—in their mania to get the work down on paper. They consume *themselves*: reminiscence is less troublesome than research, less complicated than rehashing all those tedious friends and lovers. And, once you've finished with yourself, you use whatever else happens to be at hand. A Perry Smith in Kansas, a Sook in Alabama—all grist for the mill.

It is hard to think of an odder literary pairing than *In Cold Blood* and "A Christmas Memory," one an extraordinary piece of journalism; the other a reminiscence lightly disguised as fiction. Song of experience; song of innocence. The latter is also one of the weaker exemplars of the so-called "Southern short story," an art form long held to be the personal fiefdom of Faulkner, Welty, and O'Connor. "A Christmas Memory" is undeniably pleasurable, good for a late-evening winter read—but not even close to the "world's best short story" as its author repeatedly and inanely boasted.

And yet . . . How many American writers have given a living human being to the culture: Holly Golightly? How many writers have appended phrases to the language as indelible as "Breakfast at Tiffany's" or *In Cold Blood*? In "A Christmas Memory," Capote had a fine idea for a story of childhood—then he infused it with a poetic, burnt-golden sadness. Perhaps by writing of Buddy and his aged friend, he intended to tell us that other story—of a child left alone in a New Orleans hotel room, the room-service maids and hotel employees specifically instructed to ignore the screams coming forth, which, like endless waves, battered against the ceiling and walls until eventually there was nothing but a single scream enveloping the child, until the child himself couldn't hear the sound, and only a numbing, irreversible coldness was left in its place.

Cawdor

Near the beginning of *MacBeth*, we receive one of those brief crystalline scenes that are often over-shadowed by more popular matinee moments like *"A plague on both your houses"* or *"And say besides that in Aleppo once . . ."*

The scene takes place in the aftermath of war—a war whose victor is Duncan, King of Scotland—a brief dialogue between the king and his oldest son Malcolm:

> Duncan: *Is execution done on Cawdor? Are not*
> *Those in commission yet returned?*
>
> Malcolm: *My liege,*
> *They are not yet come back. But I have spoke*
> *With one that saw him die, who did report*
> *That very frankly he confessed his treasons,*
> *Implored your Highness' pardon, and set forth*
> *A deep repentance. Nothing in his life*
> *Became him like the leaving it. He died*
> *As one that had been studied in his death*
> *To throw away the dearest thing he owed*
> *As 'twere a careless trifle.*

From the play's exposition, we learn that a certain Sweno, King of Norway, has invaded King Duncan's Scotland, abetted by two Scottish rebels, Macdonwald and Cawdor. The war, although bloody, was not a long engagement and victory went to Duncan; after which, Norway sued for peace. Meanwhile, having landed on the wrong side of history, the nobleman Cawdor is captured and executed. All of this is by way of preamble to MacBeth's receiving the title, Thane of Cawdor, as reward for his service to King Duncan. When the first Cawdor is executed, MacBeth becomes Cawdor II, and the play's main narrative commences.

But what about the original Cawdor—this back story to the play? We know almost nothing about him except the report of his death, spoken by Malcolm, who himself is reporting what someone else told him. All offstage. All second and third hand.

Why did the nobleman Cawdor throw in with Norway? We are given no evidence that Duncan was a tyrant, deserving of overthrow. More likely the opposite. Did Cawdor, like Macbeth a little later, have ambitions for the throne himself? Some long held personal motive, revenge, etc.? Was there another ambitious wife in the mix, God-help-us, another Lady MacBeth? Or was it just the usual resentment, perhaps a thwarted career? *Duncan is king by sheer luck and inheritance. I could be twice the ruler. What has he achieved that I could not surpass?*

Nevertheless, all comes to disaster. Shakespeare doesn't give us details, but we're allowed to imagine what might have happened:

Bloodied, his armies routed, Cawdor would have been manacled and brought to the king's commissioners. An impatient soldier stands behind them, with a still wet sword. These things usually take only a few seconds; the traitor forced to his knees, head bent. Perhaps because he is a nobleman, the emissaries make a token gesture: "Do you have anything to say?" The field behind them is littered with bodies, blood, limbs. To beg for mercy is useless. He has ten, maybe twenty seconds to live. The men before him have no interest in anything he might have to say or explain; they want only to get this over with and return home to their wives and families, away from the awful field.

Then Cawdor hears himself speaking:

> I have committed treason against His Highness. I alone am guilty of this crime. I conspired with Macdonwald and Norway to overthrow the king—this I did of my own will—without coercion from any other—knowing what I was doing—my offense is before me.
>
> I know that I will die here—and I know that the king has no need of my contrition—but I do truly, here on this field, before you and before God—ask his pardon. This I do only that he may be told of my words by you.
>
> If you will permit it, unloose these shackles, and I will kneel here freely. There is no need to hold me.

The king's men allow him to kneel unbound. There is a flash of steel. The body is dragged into the center of the field where a pyre will burn all night. Then the emissaries go home.

For myself, I think that everything came upon Cawdor at once—this movement of the soul that Malcolm is so astonished to report. The prisoner's hands and arms ache from the bindings. The guards walk, drag, him forward; his head bent in pain. Then he looks up and sees the two emissaries—and the king's colors—so startling against the soot and smoke and black blood.

Malcolm is careful to report the triform act of Cawdor: admission of guilt, the imploring of pardon, and profound repentance. For most men, such a transformation is usually the act and journey of an entire life, with its setbacks, failures, and unimagined turns; yet here it is condensed into the last minute of Cawdor's life.

The first part of Malcolm's speech sounds like a paraphrase, as if Malcolm were doing his best to repeat the words given him by the original witness. And that first witness, of course, goes un-named. Was he one of the king's commissioners? Did he simply report to Malcolm in a kind of official debriefing? Surely he himself was moved by Cawdor's death; nevertheless, Malcolm has absorbed the story and refracted it through his own mind and language. Malcolm reports in direct language Cawdor's transformation; then he soars into poetry with the line: "Nothing in his life became him like the leaving it."

By now, we have completely left the transcript of the original witness and we are listening to Malcolm speak as if he himself had been there, *which he had not.* The famous line lies exactly in the middle of Malcolm's speech, a summit of his poetic apprehension of the story he has been given.

Still, Malcolm's rational mind resists, cannot take all in, grapples with Cawdor's death. He says that Cawdor seemed to be throwing away his life—"a careless trifle." Is this, we wonder, a slight hint of incomprehension, a suggestion of despair, of fatalism?

How fine that Malcolm's uncertainty reflects the reader's inability to take all this in. We too struggle to comprehend. But this tiny hint of ambivalence is false, is only our insufficiency to imagine such a state of freedom—a state where the mere prolonging of one's physical existence is irrelevant, a trifle really. The speech in fact does *not* have three parts to be broken up and analyzed but a magnificent unity, and while perhaps Malcolm and we feel ourselves questioning and troubled, this very hesitation enriches the scene.

Malcolm's report of Cawdor's death leads us to envision not despair, but abandonment into providence. On a field of blood, a condemned traitor is dragged forward and thrown before the king's men. Somewhere there is a clatter of horses, fire, smoke, the crying of birds. In the last second of his life, Cawdor obtains his freedom.

Dortmunder Agonistes

Each of Donald E. Westlake's Dortmunder novels contains the same short, almost verbatim, paragraph describing the back room of the O.J. Bar & Grill in New York City, where a gang of thieves holds planning meetings. Here's a recent version from *What's So Funny?* (2007):

> Rounding the end of the bar, Dortmunder walked down the hall, past the doors labeled POINTERS and SETTERS with black dog silhouettes, and past the former phone booth, now an unoccupied sentry box containing nothing but notes to and from the lovelorn plus a few frayed wire ends, and into a small square room with a concrete floor. Beer and liquor cases were stacked against all the walls, floor to ceiling, leaving just space enough for a beat-up old round wooden table with a once-green felt top, this surrounded by half a dozen armless wooden chairs. The only light source was a single bare bulb under a round tin reflector hanging from a long black wire over the center of the table.

For Westlake addicts, this recurring paragraph is a cheerful bit of business, like a refrain in music, an acknowledgment that we are back on familiar ground. We look forward to its appearance in every new novel like a moviegoer waiting for an Alfred Hitchcock cameo.

Or, perhaps, we recognize each re-staging of the back-room scene as the author's nod to a fiction writer's perennial problem—setting forth a novel's exposition when a familiar cast of characters is carried over from one book to another. P.G. Wodehouse had to deal with the same problem:

> In recording the latest installment of the Bertram Wooster Story, a task of which I am about to have a pop, I don't see how I can avoid delving into the past a good deal, touching on events which took place in previous installments and explaining who's who and what happened when and where and why, and this will make it heavy going for those who have been with me from the start . . . On the other hand, I must consider the new customers. I can't just leave the poor perishers to try to puzzle things out for themselves.

To try to puzzle things out . . . An apt phrase which by coincidence also happens to be a perfect description of Dortmunder's daily challenge as New York's unluckiest criminal. All those never-ending obstacles and puzzles—they are the cause of Dortmunder's agony and the source of our bliss.

John Archibald Dortmunder is Westlake's gift to American humor writing, a knight-errant sent forth upon the eastern USA. A New Yorker like his creator, Dortmunder is a diehard urbanite, bonded to the city, his residence and workplace, in much the same way as his fellow boulevardiers and coevals in comic mishap, Ignatius J. Reilly and Bertie Wooster, are tied to New Orleans and London. The series occasionally roams outside the five boroughs—to Washington D.C., a castle in Scotland, a ghost town in Oklahoma, the Las Vegas strip—but would be inconceivable without its principal setting in New York. Westlake was born in Brooklyn in 1933 and relishes taking us on tours of the city: to Gansevoort Street in the West Village; up Fifth Avenue to Central Park where we can stroll among the "unicyclists, the tree worshippers, the Hare Krishnas, and the lost Boy Scout troops," then past all those buildings made of "the tannish-gray limestone New Yorkers call brownstone," then maybe over to the West Seventy-ninth Street Boat Basin, "where you could launch your boat . . . or drop an unwanted volunteer into the river and let him drift out to sea."

Dortmunder began his career in 1970 in *The Hot Rock*, a novel which, according to legend, Westlake conceived as another hard-nosed Parker novel and then developed into the first Dortmunder book when he couldn't shake off its comic undertow. (Indeed, *The Hot Rock* exists alone in a kind of Early Dortmunder Period, with one or two guns wielded and a few threats of violence, as if Westlake were working out for himself the shuffling, pure comedic lines that the series would later develop.) We meet Dortmunder on a day that he's getting out of prison. Over the course of thirteen novels (the fourteenth is due out in 2009), he somehow manages not to return to prison—although just barely. Even though the modern world encroaches on the novels—telephone booths and record players give way to answering machines and extension phones, which themselves give way to PCs, cell phones and ATMs—Dortmunder remains the same age over the course of the series. He's in his middle forties, hang-dog, lanky, forever slouching. He looks like a shoe salesman in the most demoralized outlet store in America. He was raised by nuns in an orphanage in Dead Indian, Illinois, and apparently he's never gotten over it.

At present, Dortmunder lives in an apartment in Manhattan with his lady companion May, a cashier at Safeway. May is not described in detail by Westlake (once, he mentions that she's tall and thin with graying black hair) but it's easy to imagine her as somewhat dowdy—middle-aged and unremarkable just like Dortmunder. She's a reformed chain-smoker (when she's worried, she walks around the apartment, flicking invisible ashes) and an occasional participant in Dortmunder's schemes. She's not a criminal per se, but adds to her salary at Safeway by bringing home sacks of lifted groceries every day—a perk of the job she believes she's due and one that the managers would surely have offered her if it hadn't slipped their minds.

When he is not slumped in an easy chair watching TV with May, Dortmunder is the ostensible leader of a small, loosely aligned group of New York burglars and robbers—all of whom are freelancers but who gather from time to time when a new-found caper requires a team effort.

Andy Kelp, for instance, is Dortmunder's most regular working partner, younger than John, a sharp dresser, extroverted, optimistic, as persistent as a dog nipping at your heel. In *What's the Worst That Could Happen?* (1996), Kelp takes Dortmunder to meet his new girl friend:

> Andy said, "Anne Marie, just as a hypothetical, what would you say if I told you we weren't entirely honest?"
>
> "I'd say nobody's entirely honest," she said. "What kind of not honest are you?"
>
> "Well, mostly we pick up things," he said.
>
> John said, "Right. That's it. Pick up things."
>
> She shook her head, not getting it, and Andy said, "You know, like, we see things lying around and we pick them up."
>
> Anne Marie felt her way through the maze of this locution. She didn't quite know how to phrase her next question, but went ahead anyway: "You mean . . . you mean you're thieves?"
>
> Beaming, happy she'd got it, Andy said, "Personally I prefer the word *crook*. I think it's jauntier."
>
> "You're crooks."
>
> "See? It is jauntier."

Would that it were that simple . . . what's the worst that could happen? Well, plenty. Nearly drowning in an upstate reservoir, for example, while attempting to recover a buried casket with seven hundred thousand dollars inside. Or being captured, then kidnapped, then having guns pointed at you by the very target you're trying to burgle—and this, three, four, five times in as many novels, with the barked shins, bruises, and scars to prove it. Or being forced to steal the same emerald six times in a row, because it keeps being re-stolen or lost or left behind in a jail cell by one of your own purported team members, then being forced to break *into* a police precinct via *helicopter,* as well as break into a mental hospital via locomotive, and on and on. It should be mentioned that, for the most part, a successful Dortmunder outing is one in which no one is seriously injured or gets arrested. Profits are rare. At the end of one heist, the bank building they'd stolen (yes, the entire building, a mobile home serving as a branch bank's temporary quarters) skittered off the end of a pier and sank in the Atlantic Ocean. Most of the fun in observing Dortmunder's carefully planned operations consists in waiting for the calamities to happen—Dortmunder waiting for them first of all, knowing that the worst will always happen, knowing that his plans will always end in disaster, no longer even shocked, just curious to see what variation on failure fate will play on him this time.

The pilot of that helicopter is a man named Stan Murch. Like Andy Kelp, Stan is a regular member of the crew, the gang's wheelman and automotive specialist. He claims that he can drive, steer, pilot, navigate, anything that moves, but in *The Hot Rock*, when Dortmunder sits beside him in the helicopter and watches him getting acquainted with various strange-looking knobs and gauges, a new kind of outrage washes over Dortmunder, a hitherto un-experienced fear and astonishment as if the waves of outrage he'd been experiencing heretofore and almost gotten used to, had even come to expect, were just playthings, and there were whole new worlds of disasters still to come:

> Dortmunder, suddenly suspicious, said, "You *did* drive one of these things before, right?"
>
> "I told you," Murch said. "I can drive anything."
>
> "Yeah," Dortmunder said. "That's what you told me, I remember that."
>
> "Right," said Murch. He kept grinning at the helicopter.
>
> "You *can* drive anything," Dortmunder said, "but the question is *did* you ever drive one of *these* things before?"
>
> They shut the door and Dortmunder studied Murch studying the controls. After a minute Dortmunder said in disgust, "You never even *saw* one of these things before."
>
> Murch turned on him. "Are you kidding? I read in *Popular Mechanics* how to *make* one, you don't think I can *drive* one?"

Stan lives in Canarsie in Brooklyn with his mother, Gladys, who's known in the novels as Murch's Mom (it wouldn't be advisable to call her Gladys to her face), a feisty New York cabdriver and occasional member of the crew. When they're not working, you might find Stan and his mom, of an evening, in the living room of their house in Brooklyn listening to a recording of the Indy 500. Not a video or a play-by-play commentary, but a sound recording of the race cars—engine noise, tire screeches, skids, the howl of brakes. . . beautiful tumultuous noise.

Stan owns a red blazer that he occasionally wears in midtown Manhattan when standing in front of a luxury hotel. Arriving guests not only hand over the keys to their gleaming BMWs and Lexi, but give Stan a nice tip, after which he says, "Thank you," and drives to Maximilian's Used Cars for a quick cash sale.

In *Jimmy the Kid* (1974), while killing time at a diner on Long Island, Stan happened to spot a potentially profitable sedan in the parking lot, its owner sprawled out drunk a few booths away. "Hm-mmm." At which point, an auto-dealer's car-carrier pulled into the lot with four choice Buicks. Four versus one—an easy decision for a young capitalist. Still, a shame to leave a perfectly good Continental behind. Was there room on the car-carrier for one more? Would it be possible? "Hmmmmm."

There are other associates, colleagues, part-time crew members, acquaintances: Tiny Bulcher, for example, known variously as "a man mountain," or "a mastodon in clothes" or "a man monster—or monster man," whose demeanor and temperament is that of the world's largest grenade. He's "a hillside brought to life," a piece of topography with a profoundly entrenched anger problem and currently off its meds. Also, J.C. "Josie" Taylor, Tiny's girl friend, and the owner of three mail-order scams which she runs out of the same office—a music-writing service, a detective school, and a porn business. She's also the inventor and registered lobbyist for her own fictitious island-nation, Maylohda, currently receiving seed money from a number of United Nations development funds.

In two of the novels, we meet Wally Knurr, a gentle computer nerd, four feet six inches tall and 285 pounds, who finds the love of his live, Myrtle Street, and woos her, fights for her, and even wins her!

Wally Whistler is an absentminded lockman, known for fiddling with a cage at the zoo one day and accidentally letting a lion out; also for shipping himself to Brazil via the cargo ship that he was supposed to be breaking into. Then, having the devil's own time in returning home since Brazil and the United States don't have an extradition treaty, and he "like some other of Dortmunder's friends, liked to travel by extradition."

There are other lockmen, wheelmen, utility men: Roger Chefwick, Ralph Winslow, Herman X, Fred and Thelma Lartz (a driving team; they receive only one share in any scores), Jim O'Hara, Gus Brock.

In *Nobody's Perfect* (1977), Dortmunder and Kelp visit the studio of a painter who specializes in art fraud. The painter's girlfriend and model is "a girl of about twenty curled up on the sofa, with an old plaid throw rug draped across her legs." As appreciative of beauty as the next guy, Dortmunder wouldn't mind staring at her forever and his language rises to the occasion: "She was slender, but with roundnesses and softnesses, like the world's tastiest peach, and her smile made her cheeks plump and delectable." The Dortmunder novels are neither round nor soft, but they are among the tastiest items in American comic writing. John and the gang have schemed, planned, plotted (and usually failed) to steal a little of everything—gems and jewelry, fine art, the czar's chess set, a saint's femur, Las Vegas cash, antique cars. They've gotten involved in an extortion scheme on an Indian casino; they've committed a kidnapping (during which, naturally, they were outwitted by the child-kidnap-victim at every step—they hadn't read "The Ransom of Red Chief"). They've rescued a young Catholic nun from her rich father who was attempting to deprogram her, and even stolen a bank.

For Dortmunder fans, a strange conjecture comes to mind from time to time. Just what has Donald Westlake really been up to these past thirty-nine years? Yes, he's been offering us light entertainment in a tradition that comes down straight from his predecessors, Mark Twain, P.G. Wodehouse, the Marx Brothers, and S.J. Perelman. But another possibility occurs to us: that in the guise of writing a series of picaresque crime novels, he might actually have composed a long comic poem on America, a benevolent and rollicking celebration of our multiplicity, dumbness, and native obstinacy. Westlake sings of ordinary working stiffs (who happen to be heisters), of New York streets, of sidewalks and diners, of upstate hick towns, cops, truck-drivers, husbands and wives, of a mother and son forever arguing about the quickest route from Canarsie to the O.J. Bar on Amsterdam Avenue, and of a rumpled Safeway cashier trying to cheer up her man by serving him a bowl of his favorite breakfast cereal—"Wheaties and milk and sugar, in a ratio of 1/1/1." John Archibald Dortmunder is the sourest of New York City sourballs, a grumbler and a chronic depressive, and to spend time in his company is one of the happiest things I know.

River Stories

A Mississippi River journey to the South begins in Hannibal, Missouri, and ends thirteen hundred miles away in the Gulf of Mexico in the open sea—salt and blue water—a consummation achieved after endless turns and curves on a levee-lined ribbon of brown water. Along the way, the town names are checked off like beads on a prayer string—St. Louis, Memphis, Vicksburg, Natchez, Baton Rouge, New Orleans. Familiar names, perhaps too familiar. The river, as its chroniclers tell us, meanders in time, and, if it were not for the Army Corps of Engineers and dumb luck, the Mississippi might abandon any of those famed cities as easily as it carves a fresh cutbank or spawns a new island.

Its name? . . . Derived from the Ojibwe word *misi-ziibi* (Great River) or *gichi-ziibi* (Big River); or the Algonquian *misi-sipi* (Big Water); or some such combination; or maybe from the Winnebago, Fox, Sauk, Choctaw, Chickasaw, Natchez or Yazoo, named long before the Europeans knew there was a continent lying there—in their eyes, their European eyes, a continent idle and prime for plunder—much less knew that there was a bisecting river in its interior, a mile-wide highway, north to south. It is fitting that it took a Missourian like Mark Twain, certainly no Deep South native (although he enlisted briefly in the Confederacy) yet not strictly a Northerner either, a journalist, steamboat pilot, and author, to create Huck and Jim on their wooden raft, drifting between two banks, a tiny particle of the endless bounty of the Mississippi River, which blithely carries *everything* with it—Minnesota's snow; billions of cubic feet of the several states; ten-foot catfish; every species of mammal and corpse; trees and telephone poles; railroad cars and houses—this astonishing mode of transport, catholic and indiscriminate, and not at all particular of timetables or destinations.

For example, look at 1927. The Big One: Arkansas, Mississippi, Louisiana. 27,000 square miles under water. At places, under thirty feet of water. One thousand dead; one million homeless. Among those caught up in the events, William Alexander Percy, a Greenville planter's son and a poet, found himself marshalling supplies, organizing rescues, feeding, clothing, and sheltering several thousand victims clinging to the tops of levees. His nephew and future ward, Walker, age eleven at the time, goes on to become an even greater writer, settling in New Orleans, eventually in Covington, Louisiana, across Lake Pontchartrain, both places directly in the path of whatever storms, floods, or hurricanes might decide to come that way, whether from the north like the flood of '27 or from the south like the Gulf's annual hurricanes. This nephew who, as a young man, would drive to Oxford one day to meet William Faulkner, maybe shake his hand, exchange a few words, about . . . what?, literature?, well, probably anything *but* that, (and, in fact, not even getting out of the car, as the story goes) even though the great man knew W.A. Percy, and had visited Greenville in days past to do some drinking and to play tennis, and had written his own flood story, a novella, with a young convict stranded in a wooden skiff and a pregnant woman and the smaller rivers flowing backward and a child's birth right there in the flooded Mississippi of 1927. Faulkner contrived *Old Man* (1939) as a comedy in spite of its circumstances. Its opening paragraph is a tour de force of comic invention, a paragraph of some thirty lines in two sentences, comprising a history of the convict's naïve, stumbling, youthful failed railroad robbery (he was inspired by penny-press novelettes)—an opening passage so charming that the readers of *The Saturday Evening Post*, *Harper's*, and *The Atlantic Monthly* must have relaxed for a moment and said, yes, finally, even in spite of the man's baroque reputation, here's a narrative we can actually enjoy instead of fighting tooth and nail through some intricately layered verbal maze, some insane knot of literary experimentation and obscurity. They were wrong, of course, since in no time Faulkner gave in to all his urges and let fly with one endless paragraph after another (let's face it, his subject, the Mississippi River flood, was irresistible to an epic voluptuary like Faulkner). And so, on they swept, wave after wave of prose, which is often, as much as we hate to admit it, precise, necessary, and cogent even when it seems most nearly out of control:

> But he didn't see Vicksburg: the skiff, traveling at express speed, was in a seething gut between soaring and dizzy banks with a glare of light above them but he did not see it; he saw the flotsam ahead of him divide violently and begin to climb upon itself, mounting, and he was sucked through the resulting gap too fast to recognise it as the trestling of a railroad bridge; for a horrible moment the skiff seemed to hang in static indecision before the looming flank of a steamboat as though undecided whether to climb over it or dive under it, then a hard icy wind filled with the smell and taste and sense of wet and boundless desolation blew upon him; the skiff made one long bounding lunge as the convict's native state, in a final paroxysm, regurgitated him onto the wild bosom of the Father of Waters.

And who's to say he didn't pull it off: describe the indescribable? As well as tell an exciting adventure story—readable and enjoyable by us ordinary mortals not just the fellow geniuses and literary angels who were probably Faulkner's natural constituency—about the young man caught up in comic/horrific circumstances, who simply wants to get back home, back to prison, to the prison authorities whom he believes he is required to report to in order to return the state's skiff (he'd been sent into the flood to rescue the woman); although he makes us pay for it, Faulkner does, manages to out-Absalom Absalom, and make us pay dearly for the comedy and the characters and the richly cinematic narrative.

The Percy nephew, Walker, eventually adopted Louisiana as his home state, becoming a great man himself with a string of novels, and died in 1990, thus missing by fifteen years the next Big One, Katrina, sweeping up from the Gulf that late day in August 2005, flooding the city so well known by all three. Most of the victims black, again, this time as before—homeless, flooded, drowned—who had clung to the levee-tops in 1927 and this time crowded onto the interstate overpasses and rooftops or floated out on whatever boats they could salvage, mattresses, ice chests, wooden gates—little else, it seems, having changed.

Southern boats: We still own them, dock them, drag them up from the bayous to be stored upside-down on grassy banks: flat-bottomed johnboats, twelve and fourteen feet long, on every pond and river in the South, even on the Mississippi for those daring enough, made of wood or aluminum, and strapped to the tops of cars or the beds of pickup trucks or towed on trailers—ubiquitous, invisible, prolix. Such vessels are the direct descendants of Huck and Jim's raft, which was itself derived from another river-entity, a lumber-raft, passing in the night like a floating town. A lumber-raft, we gather, is an item of river commerce, a great float of timber being hauled to market, some portion of which has come loose and proceeds on a freelance transit, until it runs aground on an island or a sand bar or someone's front porch—the story is still told around here, apocryphal no doubt, of an Ohio family preparing to relocate to Louisiana, who saw their house swept away by a spring flood, picked off its footings and now sailing down the Ohio like a steamboat, and the despairing family only able to pack up the few belongings they had managed to salvage, load up their wagon, then make their way to their new property in East Carroll Parish. Once there, while looking for a new house site, they spotted their old house on a bluff a half-mile from the river, the building upright, plumb and level, as if professional movers had set it there.

Huck and Jim had to make do with more rudimentary lodgings. Their raft: twelve feet by sixteen feet, about the dimensions of a bedroom in a ranch-style suburban house, onto which they built a wooden shelter, with a dirt floor so they could build a fire inside. A steering oar, a forked stick to hang a warning lantern for emergencies. Their possessions were a few clothes and quilts and household objects that they had scavenged from an abandoned house floating by (the house with Huck's dead Pap inside that Jim kept Huck from seeing). Would Thoreau have approved of their existence? Certainly. Traveling at night by starlight and moonlight and sleeping by day, tied up to a towhead (a tree-covered sandbar). Nor were they ignorant of the singularity of this new life, a life untethered; the two of them becoming philosophers by necessity:

> We said there warn't no home like a raft, after all. Other places do seem so cramped up and smothery, but a raft don't. You feel free and easy and comfortable on a raft.

Free and easy and comfortable, assuming you do not drown. Avoiding which is the whole point, one might say, for Huck and Jim, for the lost convict and the pregnant woman, and for you and for me; although not for Quentin Compson whose predicament the second day of June 1910 consisted precisely in finding a way *to drown*, a project which takes him most of the day, and some hundred and thirty pages of Faulkner's Quentin section in *The Sound and the Fury* (1929). Here's its famous opening, all about watches and time:

> When the shadow of the sash appeared on the curtains it was between seven and eight oclock and then I was in time again, hearing the watch. It was Grandfather's and when Father gave it to me he said I give you the mausoleum of all hope and desire; it's rather excruciating-ly apt that you will use it to gain the reducto absurdum of all human experience which can fit your individual needs no better than it fitted his or his father's.

After such an opening, it won't take the author many pages to get up to speed. To get his italics key working; to begin shifting scenes, times, voices; get his consciousness fully streaming, like water in a flooding river:

> The corridor was still empty of all the feet in sad generations seeking water. *yet the eyes unseeing clenched like teeth not disbelieving doubting even the absence of pain shin ankle knee the long invisible flowing of the stair-railing where a misstep in the darkness filled with sleeping Mother Father Caddy Jason Maury door I am not afraid only Mother Father Caddy Jason Maury getting so far ahead sleeping I will sleep fast when I door Door door*

Faulkner's Oxford is inland, far from the Mississippi River, although it is bounded by the Tallahatchie and the Yocona, both of which eventually join the Yazoo, which itself merges with the Mississippi above Vicksburg. Still, Faulkner's novel is not a river story, except in this odd digression at Harvard, 1,300 miles away. (And please note that it was Quentin who renamed his mentally handicapped younger brother Maury, the novel's title character Benjamin: "Benjamin, our lastborn, sold into Egypt".) In the end, Quentin does manage to drown himself in the Charles River in Cambridge with two six-pound flatirons in his pockets and memories of honeysuckle and sisters and bridges, and the three Northern boys fishing the river like any pack of boys anywhere in the South. Faulkner managed to tell his story, this last day of a college boy's life, with a considerable quantity of straightforward prose and narrative, even a long half-comic short story of Quentin finding a lost Italian girl at a bakery and, Southern gentleman that he is, trying to locate her parents or family or guardians or someone, anyone, to hand her over to (almost, one might say, like the convict on the Mississippi with his own superfluous companion, the pregnant woman, that he doesn't know what to do with). The narrative interspersed, however, with nothing less than an evocation of Quentin's entire psyche and unconscious, his tortuous psycho-sexual, philosophical, swirling interior existence, which Faulkner reproduces as a kind of on again/off again geyser, an uncontrollable flow of images, dreams and nightmares, as if Quentin's brain that June day contained three or four hundred simultaneously melding and diverging rivers and memory streams, which Quentin had no more control of than the young convict had control of his scudding, toppling skiff in the flooded Mississippi.

If Quentin's is a drowning story, then Ellen Douglas's "On the Lake," is a near-drowning story, an adventure tale set on a sprawling horseshoe lake of the Mississippi River (one of hundreds of such former river bends—here called Lake Okatukla, near Douglas's made-up town of Philippi, Mississippi), a horror tale deftly disguised as a balmy summer outing undertaken by thirty-six-year-old Anna Glover, a couple of her young sons, and Anna's black friend and former employee, Estella. (You're never really *scared* in Faulkner's *Old Man,* since the comic underpinnings are so strong and your gasps of awe are as much directed at the author's audacious prose style as the natural catastrophe he is so diligently describing. "On the Lake" has more in common with Lawrence Sargent Hall's "The Ledge," set in the Atlantic Ocean off Maine, the scariest water story I know.) Douglas offers us a capsized wooden skiff in the middle of a mile-wide river-lake during a thunderstorm: whitecaps, waves over the gunwales, and two women, one white, one black, bobbing in the water, the black one panicked, pulling Anna Glover under, who is trying to rescue her, who should never have let her join the fishing party in the first place—and Estella, who herself should never have joined, who cannot swim, who fears water and boats, and whose ultimate fear has come to pass this day, but who cannot be judged, as she pulls Anna down with her—just as Anna cannot be judged either, at her strength's end, when she must kick Estella away, to drown alone, if she, Anna, is to live and protect her boys, floating in their life preservers. So Anna believes that she has murdered Estella, believes it virtually until the next day in the hospital visiting the strangely undrowned Estella, after everyone has been rescued and Estella's limp body dragged to a pier, and then miraculously brought back to life, who herself that next day, cannot remember anything of the catastrophe, the flailing or the sinking, who can only *thank* Anna for saving her life, a life which Anna believes she had left to die.

In 1954, Louisiana-born Shirley Ann Grau offered *The New Yorker's* urbane subscribers a tour of a strange new world below New Orleans. Her long story "Joshua" is set during World War II when German U-boats prowled the Gulf of Mexico and even tried to nudge into the open channels of the Mississippi. Her young hero, Joshua Samuel Watkin, an eleven-year-old African-American boy, lives with his mother and father in a vast waterworld of bayous, channels, and swamps. The settlements here are black, not Cajun, although the fishermen sing French songs when they're drinking, take their pirogues into the bayous, and speak in locutions that wouldn't be out of place in Houma or New Iberia: "I don't talk in my sleep, me."

Grau sets out the boundaries of Joshua's universe in her characteristic, carefully wrought prose:

> South of New Orleans, down along the stretch that is called the Lower Coast, the land trails off to a narrow strip between river and marsh. Solid ground here is maybe only a couple of hundred feet across, and there is a dirt road that runs along the foot of the green, carefully sodded levee. . . . To the east is the expanse of shifting swamp grass, and beyond that is the little, sheltered Bay Cardoux, and farther still, beyond the string of protecting islands, is the Gulf. To the west is the Mississippi, broad and slow and yellow.

Grau's "Joshua" is not simply a river story; it is composed almost completely of water:

> For it rains almost constantly from October to March. Not hard; not a storm; there is never any lightening. There is just a steady, cold rain.
>
> Joshua turned his eyes toward the window. All he could see was gray sky. Raining, solid, gray sky in all four directions—east over the swamps and west over the river and north to the city and south to the Gulf, where the fishing boats went, and the U-boats were hiding.
>
> The wind blew in swirling eddies—like puffs of smoke, almost, the drops were so fine. Joshua rubbed the wet from his eyes. Over the noise of the rain he heard the faint sound of the river against the levee, a sound that went on day and night, winter and spring, until you got so used to it you had to make a special effort to hear it.

The faint sound of the river against the levee . . . an extraordinary line, as if the river were a great ship rubbing in its berth. I've lived over fifty years in Louisiana in a town on the Ouachita River, and never once heard such a sound or registered such an image.

As Grau traces the plot of her story, we follow Joshua in his daily rounds trudging in the mud between his parents' wooden cabin and the town's general store. The talk everywhere is of a fisherman, Jesse Baxter, who was "blown to bits" by a German sub a week ago. None of the local men will venture into the Gulf now. Joshua's father brings home a few panfish from the bayou, but mostly he drinks. Joshua's mother berates him for cowardice and asks where the next meal is coming from, asks when Joshua is going to receive a winter coat. Husband and wife battle continuously, then make up the next day, retreating to bed and sex.

Joshua is scared of the Gulf too. He has nightmares every night about the U-boat—a danger which he cannot fully visualize. He's never seen a picture of a submarine.

Then we remember that Joshua is only eleven-years-old. He accuses himself of cowardice—but we do not. To our eyes, he is estimable, already a man: capable of navigating the flare-ups and violent tempers of his parents, of finding himself a meal of leftovers at the back of the stove, of rambling with his friend and sidekick, Henry Bourgeois. The two of them have fabricated a hideout and boy's fort in an abandoned fur company's warehouse:

> In the corners of the warehouse they had found a few furs—tattered, mangy things, too poor to be sold—and they used these as seats or beds, for sometimes they slept here, too. Their families did not miss them; after all, a boy should be able to look out for himself.

The story is set during a freezing, waterlogged Louisiana winter, and indeed Joshua has to look out for himself every day. He spends most of the story outdoors in the cold rain with no warm coat, only a beat-up tarpaulin draped across his shoulders. This theme of long sought protection brings to mind Nikolai Gogol's story, "The Overcoat" (1842), often named the world's greatest short story. Near the end of Grau's story, the author will send Joshua off in a flimsy pirogue into the Gulf marshes near the mouth of the

Mississippi. Joshua is searching for fish, maybe for a few ducks to shoot, but, during his river-journey, he will finally obtain his winter overcoat via an ingenious plot twist. Independent, self-contained, dogged young Joshua is the reincarnation of Huckleberry Finn, and, in 1954, Shirley Ann Grau gave readers cause for thanksgiving with this latest American hero, this child born of the river and the sea.

3

Notes From a Past Life

A Day on the Town

It is 1959 and *Tarzan's Greatest Adventure* is playing at a theater in the town where I live in northern Louisiana. An American actor named Gordon Scott stars in the title role—although he's without his usual co-star, a chimpanzee named Cheetah. I am nine-years-old. Forty years later, I will learn that aficionados hold this particular *Tarzan* as nonpareil—a darkly brooding, psychological *Tarzan*, an existential *Tarzan*. In addition, a young Sean Connery plays one of the villains—age twenty-nine—in an early pre-Bond performance. Needless to say, none of this concerns me in 1959.

This morning, I am in the custody of my aunt, an inveterate moviegoer like myself. She is the archetypal visiting aunt, a high school teacher from Texas—divorced, in her fifties, somewhat stout, appearing in my life three times a year: summer, Christmas, and Thanksgiving. She smokes cigarettes, reads paperback novels, works crossword puzzles, plays solitaire, watches TV—simultaneously, of course. For me, she is dazzling, witty, a soft touch at the candy counter—the best of company. She teaches my brothers and me to play Scrabble, Hearts, Canasta; teaches us the story of the Alamo, Davy Crockett, Jim Bowie. She has never learned to drive. She served in World War II as a WAC, stationed in Australia and

New Guinea, and tells me that she prays I never, ever, have to go to war, tells me that as far as she is concerned, all that the so-called Good War did was take young men and train them to be murderers. She will go with me to any movie, any time, anywhere—and this morning we've been dropped off downtown, in front of the theater. It's eleven in the morning, but no need to worry about lunch, we can fill up on popcorn. Afterwards, we're responsible for getting ourselves home on the bus.

The theater has a 1930s-style outdoor ticket booth as well as movie posters in glass display cases: *Ben-Hur, The Shaggy Dog, Gidget.* The entryway is a kind of semi-circular outdoor foyer. You can browse the movie posters just by taking two steps off the sidewalk—like window-shopping, a favorite pastime of my family. Inside, an angular, slightly scary woman patrols the aisles with a flashlight. She's an older, far less pretty version of the solitary usher in the Edward Hopper painting, "New York Movie." There are cushioned seats, two balconies, curtained boxes on left and right like an opera house. The lights dim. We watch cartoons, a newsreel, the coming attractions, finally the feature itself—Technicolor jungles, cliffs, rivers, revenge.

Afterwards, the blinding Louisiana sunlight stops us dead in our tracks. It's necessary to pause a minute in the theater foyer to squint and regain our equilibrium—a time to examine other movie posters—John Wayne, Audrey Hepburn, Doris Day. My aunt clears her throat, lights a Pall Mall. Shoppers hurry past us, men and women with serious faces. The men all wear suits and hats. Who are all these people on their urgent, frenetic courses? They're completely unreal to us, my aunt and me, after the hyper-reality, the movie-ecstasy, we have just experienced.

We're hungry after the movie—the popcorn hasn't filled us up after all. Around the corner from the theater is a department store with a diner on the first floor and a painted sign above the door: *Air-Conditioned Inside.* We walk down a side street past the back entrance to the kitchen, from which pours an inviting assemblage of aromas—hamburgers, waffles, bacon, French fries—a mélange of scent-molecules which resides permanently on this short half-block. Maybe the buildings prevent olfactory dispersion—whatever the case, when you walk down the block, it's like walking through a pleasure dome of lunch-counter delicacies. Once inside, we scramble to find an empty booth, throwing ourselves onto seats opposite each other, reaching for menus like debonair restaurant-goers everywhere—this middle-aged teacher and her nephew with the crew-cut and Bermuda shorts. A waitress appears, all starch and apron. A lifetime later, my hamburger arrives—meat and bread only. My aunt's burger drips and spills with mayonnaise, mustard, ketchup, lettuce, tomato, pickle, onion, but she makes no comment on my boring, impoverished taste.

After lunch, we pay a visit to my grandmother, in her insurance office on the eleventh floor of the bank building, the tallest and grandest edifice in town. In 1959, the city's downtown has not died yet. Parking spots are hard to find. Sidewalks are crowded with shoppers, business people, commuters at bus stops. There are banks, hotels, churches, a synagogue, hospital, restaurants, clothiers, train station, a Western Union (where I once sent a telegram to some relative in Shreveport or Chicago. True! And this was not the 1890s or 1920s but the 1950s), a library, post office, courthouse, and best of all, a gimcrack novelty shop on a side street, emporium of my secret desires—joy-buzzers, gory thumbs, rubber snakes, fly-in-the-ice-cubes.

It is the train station, however, that my aunt loves, with its intricate time-tables, stacks of luggage, smell of diesel. Anyone in town can walk two blocks and catch a daily train to Jackson, Mississippi, then on to Chicago or St. Louis. Our linkage to these cities is actual not abstract. I exist, my aunt tells me, in a universe far greater than this tiny burg, this river town in Louisiana. Besides Texas, she has lived in Washington, D.C., Nebraska, south Louisiana, San Francisco, New York City. In an antechamber next to the bank lobby, we pass a newsstand just like the ones in the movies—bulging with raucous wares. It looks as if it could fall over at any minute, filled with the substance of urbanity: magazines and newspapers, cigars, cigarettes, candy, gum, aspirin, toothpicks, maps, nail clippers, LSU football pennants, digestive aids. Somehow, at age nine, I realize that all of this richness—the sights and wonders of downtown—is being *given* to me by my aunt.

The elevator has two doors: a metal-grill affair, then a more solid one. Both are manipulated by the elevator operator, a black man, who wears a crisp, vaguely military uniform. He recognizes my aunt and the two of them speak for a moment while I press myself against the back wall. Above the door is a clock which is not really a clock—it has only one hand, a short metal arm that clicks and wobbles from numeral to numeral, never quite landing at an exact ***6*** or ***8*** or ***10***; i.e. until the elevator arrives at its corresponding floor in a kind of final shudder, and you step across a one-inch separation, and steal a glance downward through the awful gap—exactly like looking out a car window while stopped on a bridge, peering downward through the metal grates, seeking the dark universe below, terrifying, irresistible, flowing. The elevator operator has a tiny fold-down seat in one corner of the elevator, and he alone pushes the levers and turns the knobs which transport his clanking gondolier from floor to floor.

In my grandmother's narrow office—wooden file cabinets, Dickensian account books—I run straight to the window, which is dangerously shockingly open, to peer out, to search a mile away for the miniature version of my house (until my aunt and grandmother fly after me, close the window, threaten me with instant death to even *think* of taking one step closer). I know that somewhere in the distance, one of those Monopoly houses is *my* house, my back yard, my room. But how to mark off the steps, how to calibrate the distance, between these two irreconcilable spheres of existence?

My grandmother's hair is gray. She's dressed in a dark blue, pebbly-looking suit and square, dark shoes. She's the accidental inheritor of this one-room business. Did she choose such a vocation? Or is she simply holding things together for a few years, keeping the books in order, until another company will buy the business, absorb my late grandfather's small list of clients? After ten or so minutes chatting with my aunt, my grandmother smiles, hugs me warmly, kisses my cheek (her face is powdery and dry), tells my aunt and me goodbye, and then at the last second, gives me a fifty-cent piece to debauch myself with at the candy counter downstairs. In a few years she will retire to a small house, grow older, grayer, frailer, one day fall onto a bedroom or kitchen floor and break her hip, move to a nursing home, die.

My aunt died in 1984 in California, long-retired from teaching, living out her Social Security years with one of my cousins. In those years, she came to Louisiana only rarely, i.e. until her last trip by airplane, to be buried beside my grandmother and grandfather, my mother, my other aunts and uncles, neighbors and friends—in short, everyone she ever knew here. And, of course, the old downtown disappeared also, like the business districts in every small and mid-sized Southern town from the Carolinas to Texas. Was there a universal termination date announced by some central office of abandonment? November 1958? July 1959? All premises to be vacated; all structures razed.

During the ride home after visiting my grandmother, we sit near the front of the bus. My aunt is talking to an acquaintance she has just run into. Or maybe talking to the bus driver or a stranger—she will talk with anyone, white, black, stranger, friend—an ease and garrulousness acquired from years of riding Greyhounds coast to coast. The Louisiana heat along with the rumble and sway of the bus would ordinarily rock me to sleep against her, except that I want to revisit *Tarzan* in my mind. The bus-ride home always does this—evokes in me a replaying of whatever movie I've just seen. Scene by scene, I roll the plot through my brain, reliving Gordon Scott's jungle-acrobatics, his battles with lions and human villains. I do not have the words to say so, but I know that some secret knowledge has been passed on to me by my aunt concerning pleasure—movies, hamburgers, train stations, newsstands—concerning plenitude, one of the names for joy.

A Concise History of Country Music

Aberdeenshire, Scotland (*C.* 1640–1680)

During a particularly harsh and lonely winter on the moor, widower and peat-collector Hamish of Gairgowrie composes "Will Ye Come Nae More Wi' Thi' Whiskey," which becomes the first hit single of the Highland period.

The Battle of Lochballabairnben (1728)

Haughty, proper-speaking, fashion-obsessed English Army beats the ever-living hell out of combined Scotch-Irish forces and instigates the second Gaelic Migration: twenty to thirty thousand sour-faced, ex-kilt-wearing, ex-soldiers—plus their wives and children—who cross the Atlantic and settle in the Parstonial Mountain region of the future USA, and immediately turn to singing, fiddle-playing, flings, jigs, and the practice of "meadow sighing"—an intense close-harmony vocalization, used to induce childbirth, curse enemies, and peel bark off of trees. (See *Folklore and Hollows*, Glenfallan Press, 1956.)

Classic Period (1877–1939)

Jeremiah Kilgrasian (b. Argyll, North Carolina, 1909) marries Rondalene Campbell in 1936 and forms the Kilgrasians, the preeminent husband and wife duo of the American era. Jeremiah is songwriter and lead singer of the pair, with Rondalene (1916–1939) on banjo, guitar, fiddle, mandolin, euphonium, and melodo-harp.

Tragically, the duo's career ends with Rondalene's death at age twenty-three after the birth of their fourth child. An attempt to revive the Kilgrasians with Jeremiah's second wife, Dardenelle, doesn't get off the ground, nor do attempts in later years with his third and fourth wives. Still, Jeremiah writes more than 300,000 songs—a handful of which become standards, including:

"You're Gonna Do What I Say," "I Just Want to Sleep, All Right?" and "I'm Going Out for a While."

The Corandolier

A stringed instrument popular among one of the twelve splinter factions of the Steele Mountain Cherrywine School. It is believed to be a cross between a lute and an ox skull; however musicologists do not agree on its appearance, sound, or mode of playing, since no examples survive.

Late Classic Period (1939–1940)

The Cappy Wilkins era. (See NOVELTY ACTS AND CLOWNS.) After a hardscrabble childhood spent in foster homes and reform school, Clarention "Cappy" Wilkins is discovered by manager Barston Trueblood in Null, Alabama, while employed as a gas-station attendant. Trueblood sees potential in the exuberant young Wilkins and helps develop his signature "banjo bonfire" routine, which thrills audiences from New York to California during the pyrotechnic craze of the 1930s. Cleared of most charges in the Orange County Range Fire, Wilkins goes on to have a successful career in the small-loan business.

World War II

The Kiley Moon years (b. Delmore, Florida, 1922). Composer and pianist Moon bursts onto the country scene during the short-lived "Philharmonic" era, when he forms Kiley Moon and the Savannah Strings, a 250-piece ensemble, immediately recognizable by their crimson jackets, epaulets, and onstage cocktails. Moon's theme song, "Champagne Cabin," sells two million copies the first month it is released, and the Strings receive tumultuous receptions from Tartan Hill, Virginia, to Acorn, Louisiana. Whether from stubbornness, naiveté, or blackouts, Moon fails to pick up on evolving musical tastes, which are moving away from the strings and woodwinds he so loves toward the raucous brass notes of the newfound Alabama Backhoe sound. Kiley Moon and the Savannah Strings go the way of the Puerto-Rican Long-nosed Bat—and Moon eventually sells his grand pianos and emigrates to Caithness, Arkansas, where a small contingent of fans provide him with an apartment and three square meals a day until his death in 1985.

The 1950s

Dominant artist: Sylvannia Bundine (b. Rareback, Tennessee, 1938). A melodic, lilting soprano, Bundine is discovered at age seventeen singing Christmas carols in her father's dry-goods store by Angevin record producer Cornelius Lear. After careful negotiations with her father, Lear guides the shapely young Sylvannia into the glittering country-music world of the 1950s—arranging for her appearance as the Tennessee Milkmaid. Her first million-seller, "Heaven in a Hay Loft," is believed to have caused the 1955 Saltpeter Riots at Fort Tremaine, Georgia. Known for her farm-girl outfits and her Bourbon Street–inspired dance routine, the teenager "with the sky-blue eyes" goes on to record "Pastures Afar," "Potluck Supper," and everyone's favorite, "Kittens on the Back Porch, Puppies in the Yard." Unfortunately, when she turns eighteen, Lear decides that she has lost the magic of her early years, terminates her contract, and drops her off at the first bus station he comes to.

1960s

No country singer ranked higher in the 1960s than Caige Blazeman. Ruggedly handsome in his trademark red, white, and blue Stetsons, Caige scored his first chart-topper in 1968 with "You May Be KIA, But You're Still a Buddy to Me," and from there he went on to record a string of million-sellers ("Ballad of an M16," "Blessed Lord, Blessed Bullets," and "Say That Again and I'll Stomp Your Face"). He soon made his way to Hollywood, where he starred in *Twelve-String Soldiers*, a film tribute to all singers and artists who are unable to serve in uniform because of bad backs, poor eyesight, or other legitimate maladies. In recent years, Caige has performed exclusively on military bases and patriotic venues.

Railroading

Railroading or "boxcar roulette." A short-lived genre practiced in the 1980s by Blackjack Dawkins, Maynard "Rainbow" Sloan, and the Parchment Brothers. In its original form, Railroading involved enormous quantities of cocaine and lying between train tracks to hear the sounds as a line of freight cars rushed above. Of its practitioners, only Tommy-Boy Parchment survived the 1980s. He is currently studying law at his home in Morville Federal Correctional Center, Morville, Texas.

1990s to the Present

Chartreuse Di Prantano (b. Orkney Beach, California, 1980). Former lead singer for the Baltorelle Family and reigning diva of the popular new "Celtic-originalist" country sound. The Baltorelles of La Sola, California first came into prominence during the Mountaineer revival of the late 1990s. Formed by healers Norvil and Rosalie Baltorelle, the group expanded in 1997 to include sons Orion and Nebulus; their neighbors' daughters, Mauve and Chartreuse; three cousins from Napa Valley; and some kid from Fresno who owned an amplifier. After striking out on her own, Chartreuse first hit pay dirt with the famous single "Tidebeams and Moonwaves," featuring her unique canyon-yodels and improvisations on the harmonica. According to most sources, Chartreuse discovered both the title and idea for the song—which she believed would be a perfect fit for the La Sola surf crowd—in a classified ad in *MovieDreams Magazine*. In her recently published autobiography, *Auras in Flight*, Chartreuse reveals that she has sometimes questioned the country label applied to her: "Have you ever, like, *seen* a map of Kentucky and Tennessee? There's no beach for miles. That's just weird. I'm sorry."

French Baseball

In 1974, when I was twenty-four, I had the rare good luck to spend six months with a family in France. That era was probably the last hurrah for a certain picturesque notion of France, the one from your high school grammar book, with little Paul and Paulette trotting off to *école*, with old men playing *boules*, with francs instead of euros, and with the sighting of an occasional beret. It was an age before the French discovered McDonald's, Disneyland, and supermarkets the size of airplane hangars.

The Thomas's lived in the *département* of Vendée, half a mile from a village named Montournais, a traditional French town centered upon a stone church and a village square. Downtown Montournais had a bakery, two small grocery stores, a butcher shop, hotel, several cafés, a town hall, and a fish monger. Madame Thomas shopped at three or four stores each day, sometimes *each meal*, gathering fresh ingredients for dinner.

Just outside the family home was a vegetable garden—Monsieur Thomas's pride—lettuce, tomatoes, green beans, cucumbers, and onions picked daily for the evening meal. From the garden, I could see a soccer field belonging to a nearby school (where Monsieur Thomas was professor of English), could hear the cries and shouts of the players. In other directions I saw farmland, gently rolling fields, small stands of trees. Across one field was a dairy farm, owned by two brothers who were close friends of the family. We ate cheeses of the region, fresh farm eggs, milk from cows we knew by sight.

My first Saturday in France, I unveiled my secret plan: a baseball game to be played on the school soccer field. The week before I left America, I had trawled garage sales and flea markets and collected a team's worth of used bats, balls, and mitts, all stowed in an Army duffle bag. At the time, I wasn't sure what I was planning to do with my trove of equipment, but today, finally, I decided it was a good day to teach the pastime to my new friends.

As in any sandlot game in America, I first commandeered some spare shirts and jackets, and folded them into squares for use as base pads. Monsieur Thomas led his children onto the field while a crowd of neighbors and onlookers watched me stake out the bases.

Now I unbuckled the duffle bag and passed out the mitts and balls. This was extremely interesting to the French—the oddest objects they had ever seen. No, Sophie, that is not a *chapeau*. It goes on your hand. Your left hand. About then, some of the older boys left off their soccer-kicking and joined the tryouts.

I designated myself pitcher, manager and captain, and appointed the most athletic-looking of the teenagers as infielders: première, secondaire, troisième. The little ones I sent to the outfield, which I considered the safest place for them. Six or seven outfielders in all. Monsieur Thomas wanted to bat first, so I arranged him at home plate, batting right-handed. When I went into my windup, however, he had turned ninety degrees and was now facing me, as if planning to use the bat like an axe.

No, no, I explained, you must turn sideways to me. Swing the bat as if you were swinging a tennis racket. This explanation was not sufficient. His rational French mind seemed to judge that if someone was throwing a ball at you, you should face *into* that direction in order to gauge speed and angle; and I wasn't able to marshal any intelligent answers to contradict him. Look, I finally said, do it this way because I say so. And the right hand goes on top. I don't know why. Just because it does.

First pitch: a soft lob.

First swing: strike one.

Still—by what I could only gather was some Gallic love of paradox, Monsieur Thomas's lunge and miss lifted his spirits. Perhaps it was the sheer challenge of the thing: "This small sphere is attempting to pass by me . . . and I am going to hit it. *Frapper la balle!*" By now children, neighbors, uncles, everyone seemed to be getting into the spirit of the game, and I had to remonstrate with my fielders to remain at their positions, to be ready for a base hit, ready to chase down a hot grounder and throw it to whatever base I would point to.

Next half a dozen pitches: all misses.

I decided to forego the three-strike rule as a gesture of international goodwill and also because Monsieur Thomas wouldn't give up his time at bat.

Finally the miracle occurred. As my latest pitch drifted across the plate, Monsieur Thomas made contact. Not just contact, but a decent fly ball into left-center, causing my fielders to scatter like quail. Monsieur Thomas had hit the sweet spot, without even knowing what the sweet spot was. And everyone heard the beautiful sound: the crack of the bat! As unmistakable a piece of pure American bliss as was ever heard in the Republic of France.

Run! I shouted. No, not to third. To first, that way. Off he went. Meanwhile I called to my outfielders: *Allez, allez.* Go get the ball. No, not you *Monsieur,* I shouted, keep running, keep running.

A last image of the game rises in my memory, probably a dream. Well, perhaps it doesn't matter . . . *Somehow* . . .

Somehow, on that summer day thirty-four years ago, the ball has ended up in my hands, and I spot Monsieur Thomas rounding third, heading for home with a determination that I don't know the source of.

If I can beat him there, I can apply the tag. Now everyone stops and watches. They don't know the rules, don't understand what is going on, but they can tell that something is coming to a head, in this very moment, in this climactic race to home of runner and fielder.

Monsieur Thomas stretches to touch base.

I dive for the plate.

I score it an in-the-park home run. Give myself an error for missing the tag. Ring up the game as a 1-0 victory for France, and we all head home for a two-hour lunch.

Fastened

My grandfather's office stapler was a classic Swingline #4, the size of a camshaft. It resided on a heavy, phenomenally overladen oak desk, along with stacks of ledger books, pens, letters, and envelopes, and a 1929 adding machine—an apparatus as crammed and turreted with levers, buttons, keys, and gears as the German Enigma cipher machine during World War II.

Office staplers of that era had flat black surfaces, a wide pedestal base, and an unmistakable report—a kind of sharp chewy metallic scrunch, which was composed of the stapler arm's abrupt impact, the quick piercing of four or five pieces of paper, the bending of the staple's two metal tangs, and the hinge of the pivot spring snatching the arm back up in a hundredth of a second to a set, reloaded position.

I've owned a number of staplers over the years. Most of them, naturally, are broken and inhabit a desk drawer with a few half-empty boxes of staples. This is my dead stapler bin, since none of staples fits the unbroken tools, no matter how many times I try to mix and match them.

Then there are staple guns. Sears, Arrow, Bostitch—one-handed little pistols guaranteed to produce carpal tunnel syndrome in no time at all. I've watched workmen use them to install acoustic ceiling tiles, stapling through the little fins of each tile directly into pine laths, or, with a glop of adhesive, onto a Sheetrock ceiling.

Mostly though, workmen around here use staple guns to repair screen doors and windows, sometimes whole screen porches—a maintenance project recommended every decade or so in Louisiana. Our state's Amazonian climate is a repairman's dream: In only a year or two, your recently completed house project is guaranteed to begin peeling, rusting, mildewing, or decaying.

To repair a new screen porch, you first remove the thin white lattice strips that cover the screening at each frame point. These lattice strips mask the joints and create the pleasing geometric designs everyone associates with a back porch: diamonds, diagonals, ladder-backs, or plain rectangles.

Because they are brittle and old, nearly all the lattice pieces break when you remove them. Underneath the lattice lies the screen itself, stapled to the frame. You use pinchers to dispose of whatever brads remain in the frame—rusty little nails, sometimes broken and barely visible in the gray/brown surfaces. The exposed surface of the wood frame is an archeology of past screen jobs—remnants of copper, steel, aluminum screening, of ancient dried blood from some previous carpenter's thumb, of bug parts, leaves, and tiny mountain ranges of paint stubble where the lattice has tried to pull away from the frame in the long Louisiana summers.

Now you rip the sheets of screening from the frame in vertical batches—with greasy dust flying in your face. Then you roll the old screen into bats and tie the bats with hay twine for disposal. The bow ties made by the twine resemble a Hotchkiss 120 office stapler—specifically the indentation in the metal base where each staple meets its fate so to speak.

[But who was it who invented the lozenge shape of the indentation—a sort of concave double lozenge—the perfect design to coax the twin prongs of the staple inward and create the staple's classic double clasp? Eli Hotchkiss of the Hotchkiss Co.? Uri Geller? Not only do the two prongs bend perfectly toward each other (and do so in millions of repetitions) but they *curve*, in doing so. In other words, the act of bending a staple at the base plate does not just create a useful quick clamp like this: . The two prongs actually curve upwards toward the papers they just pierced—piercing them once more from the back side like this: . Take a look at some de-stapled papers: there are four pinpricks, not just two. Now look at the indentation lozenges on your stapler base. There are no flat surfaces, but rather a beautiful sculpturing of complex curves—allowing, demanding, that the two tangs achieve their intended positions.]

Shorn of its screen wire, the naked framework of a back porch is eerie, like a house with its roof taken off. This is a good time to watch a workman loading his staple gun with fresh ammunition, taking a few practice shots.

Next comes a critical moment in the project—the unrolling of the new screen wire. The workman pushes any stray patio chairs or picnic tables out of his way to clear an area in the back yard. He then holds the free end down with a scrap of wood and begins stretching out the roll. But, invariably, before he can finish rolling out the wire, the end, held down by the piece of wood, suddenly comes loose and begins to curl—a long metallic carpet shimmying all over the lawn, twisting itself into crazy knots and wrinkles—a huge mess that wraps around the workman's legs and catches him in his own trap.

With an embarrassed smile, he looks around, hoping that no one has noticed that he's fastened himself to the backyard.

The Parking Lot

In the 1970s, when I was in my twenties living in a small town in Louisiana, I took a walk every day, logging six or seven miles per trip. The neighborhood I lived in was an aging, unfashionable suburb, and to get anywhere I had to cross U.S. Highway 80, a two-lane relic from the Pre-Interstate Age, which ran through the center of town in its long curling transit from Savannah, Georgia, to Dallas, Texas. Highway 80 was a once-famous, once-formidable thoroughfare that had apparently been designed with the goal of passing every beer joint, barbecue shack, and bait stand in the Deep South.

If I didn't get killed crossing Highway 80, I could choose from a handful of circuits, all of which I knew by heart. The tours were not much different one from the other—a succession of apartment complexes, trailer parks, and G.I. houses fronted with unraked yards and identical pickup trucks either undergoing repair or bit by bit translating themselves into rust.

One afternoon, when I was at the halfway mark of a tour, just about to make the turn for home, something caught my eye in a parking lot to my right. The parking lot belonged to an apartment complex—two long rows of buildings stretching away from my path. Why did I stop? I don't know. But in the corner of my eye, I spotted a child—one- or two-years-old—moving quietly among the rows of parked cars.

I took another look. I think that my mind used about three and a half seconds to process the pieces of information I was dealing with: 1) I was twenty-six-years-old, unmarried, and untrained in any form of childcare. 2) I was taking an ordinary walk on an ordinary Tuesday afternoon. 3) I was quite certain that the community of men, women and children I lived among didn't have the slightest need or interest in anything I might have to say, think, or do.

This kid, in short, was not my responsibility. Doubtless, its parents were only a few feet away and would gather him/her up in the next second, with a word of scolding, and all would be right with the world.

I gave a third look and saw that the child was approaching the open gate of the apartment swimming pool.

O.K. O.K., I thought. Neither the narrative of my life nor the contour of my day would be greatly affected if I trotted half a dozen steps to the parking lot to give a quick wave to the youngster's parents, who, I was still convinced, were already coming out of a door, setting up the Hibachi in front of their apartment—after which I would receive a wry word of acknowledgment for my trouble: "Kids . . . Turn your back one second and they're a mile away."

I walked up to the swimming pool entrance and blocked the child from making any further headway. My young friend was a boy, I think. Wearing white underpants, no shirt, no shoes or socks. He stopped before me and looked up.

"Hello," I said. "Er, uh, say, young man, do you happen to know where your parents are?" . . . No answer. It was possible that the youngster didn't know how to speak.

All this time, I was straining my neck up and down the parking lot, hoping that someone would appear, a neighbor, a yardworker, anyone. But there was no one in sight, and by now my young charge had turned away from the swimming pool and taken off in the direction of the street. I overtook him at the edge of the street. "Sir," I continued, "Now look here. This simply will not do."

He looked at me again with a gaze of serene indifference and then reached up and took my hand. At this point, I spotted a laundromat across the street; it was one that I had used from time to time. O.K. I thought, maybe the little runaway had come from there: An overworked mother changing wash loads. Her attention flags . . .

Naturally, there was no one in the laundromat, so we returned to the apartment complex.

How had I gotten into this mess? I wondered. And how was I to get rid of this unwanted ward? There were no cell phones in those days. And the entire neighborhood seemed to be weirdly deserted. Of course, any sane mother, grandmother, or aunt would have instantly hoisted the toddler on her hip and gone from apartment to apartment, rapping on doors until the case was solved, but, well, all I can say is that I was too dumb, too young, too unmarried, and too male to envision such a step.

Finally, someone emerged from one of the apartments—a man walking to his car. "Sir, sir," I called out. "Uh, do you know where this kid belongs? I found him wandering around the parking lot. Uh, you see, I'd just would like to get him home, you know."

"No idea," he said and drove away.

In Part Two of *The Sound and the Fury*, Harvard undergraduate Quentin Compson finds a lost Italian girl in a suburb of Boston and spends ten or twelve pages trying to return her to her family. He is a Southern gentleman alone in the faraway north and for his troubles he is eventually attacked by the girl's brother, accused of kidnapping, arrested, and nearly killed by a mob. Lord, I thought, was some bizarre repetition taking place? Or was this all a dream? How was I to get rid of this damn kid?

A post office truck entered the parking lot just then. A female letter-carrier got out, with a leather bag full of mail. My friend and

I trotted up to her, "Excuse me, ma'am. This child seems to be lost and I was wondering . . ."

She didn't break stride, offered me a world-weary glance and a sigh: "Last building on the left. Upstairs. There's a whole crew of 'em always getting loose."

We made our way down the row of apartment buildings. Sure enough, at the end, I spotted an upstairs door partly ajar. I could hear the twang and crash of stereo music even from where I stood. As we mounted the metal stairs (my associate going slowly—utilizing a kind of crawl-and-pause movement), it seemed the child knew he was home.

For a moment, I considered letting him make the last few steps on his own, but then I reasoned that since I had come this far, I might as well make sure he was safely home. The two of us stood at the doorway as another blast-wave of music emerged from inside. I rapped on the door jamb. For some reason, my friend stayed at my side. Soon, on its own, the door began to open wider. I could see four or five tow-headed children and infants here and there about the living room, as well as an entwined couple lying on a couch.

She was a dishwater blonde, twenty-something, a dead ringer for the crowd of children—I wasn't too sure about the male. Was he the father? Boyfriend? Or what? He gave me a look of astonishment, affront, and hostility as the mother uncoiled herself and walked toward my friend and me.

I began my speech of explanation, feeling pretty good about myself. The crisis was over; I was a hero. I was about to witness a mother and child reunion—the most beautiful of human rites. In spite of the apartment music, a heavenly choir seemed to be singing somewhere just behind and above me. Could there be a civic commendation in my future? A photo with the mayor?

I opened my mouth to speak but was not able to complete a single word, before the young woman grabbed the child by the arm, jerked him into the apartment, and slammed the door in my face.

Thirty years have gone by since that day.

I haven't given my young friend much thought during those years, I have to admit. Of course, today, in hindsight, I know that I should have phoned the police about the young mother—her criminal parenting. (But why hadn't the letter-carrier done anything?) Today, I know better, having seen dozens of television specials. I can only plead ignorance, innocence, and apathy—standard traits of a twenty-six-year-old in those ancient days of the 1970s.

And where is he now, my momentary ward?

I still take a daily walk, in a neighborhood not far from that of the 1970s. I live in the same town, a member of the same blue collar community—hell, I make about the same salary. My friend would be thirty-two or thirty-three today. Is he the internist working up my annual physical at the public hospital I go to? Or is he the mechanic at my garage? Is he the city cop who gave me a ticket in a speed trap last Thanksgiving? Is he my Republican state representative dedicated to family values? Is he dead in Iraq?

Last week, a thirty-two-year-old man drove to his in-laws' house a block from where I live. He shot and killed his estranged wife and mother-in-law, wounded his father-in-law, and then fired a number of shots into the neighborhood, while his children fled to nearby houses. Then he holed himself up in the house and killed himself.

A north Louisiana man. Hunter and gun owner. A man of the South. The police report said that he had been beating his wife and children for years. In fact he'd been arrested a few hours before, at midnight, at the same house, for disturbing the peace and for threatening to kill his wife and everyone there. Arrested, booked, jailed, bonded-out, released. (The paperwork on his wife's latest restraining order hadn't gone through.) Then he went to his home in an adjoining parish, picked up his guns and came back and did what he said he was going to do.

Was *this* my young friend?

I think of those shotgun and rifle rounds spraying the neighborhood, one block from the route I take every morning. How easy it would have been for a random shot to have dropped me dead on my ordinary morning walk.

Is there a thread, as the old story says, that weaves all our lives together? Is the lost child in the parking lot the wretched murderer a block from my house? Or is he a poet? When I used to take my walk all those years ago, I passed a live oak that my landlady told me was standing when Indians lived in this region hundreds of years ago. Those first residents—ethnically-cleansed by my European ancestors. My own ancestors who, in turn, imported Africans a few years after that to work the fields I pass through today, fields which are now rows of houses instead of rows of cotton. Africans, who, from time to time, were lynched by my ancestors, perhaps, in the same oak tree that the Indians saw. All along the path of my morning walk, there's not a step I take that's not soaked in blood.

A North-South Story

Sam Humphrey had to look twice. A name he hadn't seen in fifty years had just appeared on a military plaque outside his window. The window of a sightseeing bus, making a tour of the Corregidor battlefield in the Philippines.

The name was Capt. Samuel McReynolds, U.S. Army, commander of an artillery battery on Corregidor in 1941 and 1942, before the island fortress fell to the Japanese after Pearl Harbor.

Humphrey had never met Captain McReynolds, but he had known the young officer's father, Samuel McReynolds, Sr., of Monroe, Louisiana. In fact, Humphrey and his wife had lived for a month with the McReynolds in their home on the Ouachita River in Monroe.

In 1945, Humphrey was a recently-commissioned lieutenant in the Army Air Corps. A native of Connecticut, he had gone south to Louisiana to train at Selman Field Navigation School. During World War II, the small town of Monroe was the site of the country's largest navigation school—housing, training, and commissioning over 15,000 young officers who would go on to log millions of hours in Europe and the Pacific.

After earning his navigator's wings in January 1945, Humphrey was given fifteen days leave while awaiting orders. He decided to take the train home to Canton Center, Connecticut, to see his fiancé Mary. While there, he and Mary got married. Like thousands of other young American couples, they had been postponing marriage during the war years—now, still puzzled as to what course to take and without any concrete knowledge of what Sam's orders would be, they decided to take the plunge.

Thus, the young bachelor-officer Sam Humphrey, who had left Louisiana in January 1945, returned in February as a married man with his bride at his side. The two of them wanted to spend as much time together as possible before Lieutenant Humphrey received his orders. For the first few days, the newlyweds lived in a hotel in downtown Monroe. Humphrey took the bus each morning to the air base on the outskirts of town and returned each evening. But hotel life was expensive for a young lieutenant, and Humphrey told himself that he had to find an affordable apartment or boarding house—and he had to find one soon.

One day, he and Mary were strolling through Monroe's small downtown and they walked past the First Methodist Church. A group of men were talking on the church steps and Humphrey decided to ask them if they knew of any housing available to soldiers.

One of the church elders took the time to speak with the Humphreys. After a few moments, he said he believed he knew just the answer: "Why don't you go up on Riverside Drive and see Mrs. McReynolds? She's been saying she ought to rent a room to some of you service people."

The Humphreys took a bus straight there and met Mrs. McReynolds and made arrangements to take a room. Then, a few moments later, the same man they had spoken with on the church steps strolled through the front door—he was Mr. McReynolds—and he greeted them with a wry smile. McReynolds was seventy-two-years-old, a father and grandfather, and owner of a local insurance agency. To their further astonishment, as the Humphreys prepared to return to the Virginia Hotel to pick up their bags and suitcases, McReynolds "took out his car keys and handed them" to Humphrey, saying, "Here, take my car."

The Humphreys lived with the McReynolds for a full month in 1945. In effect, they spent the first weeks of their married life (their sixty-one-year marriage) as the guests of a Southern family in a small town in Louisiana. They learned that the McReynolds' four children were all grown, had left home. The only son, the youngest, was a West Point graduate, an army artillery captain. Samuel, Jr. had shipped out to the Philippines before America entered World War II, as part of Gen. Douglas McArthur's Far East forces.

When Pearl Harbor was attacked, the McReynolds family understood clearly that Samuel, Jr. was in harm's way. They followed the war news closely in those early months of 1941-42, and they feared the worst when the Philippines fell.

Then one day a message came: Captain McReynolds was missing in action.

No further information had come by 1945 when the Humphreys lived on Riverside Drive. Sam Humphrey didn't try to press Mr. McReynolds on this—a father's silence was enough.

Eventually, Lieutenant Humphrey's orders came through. He was shipped to the Pacific; his wife Mary returned to Connecticut.

Humphrey went on to fly missions in the Pacific Theatre during the last months of the war in 1945. His flights included 110 hours of combat time, for which he was awarded the Air Medal. Plus a bronze star for each of the five Pacific campaigns he served in. He was among the early contingents of Americans to land on the Japanese mainland at the end of hostilities, even before the surrender was signed. At the end of the war, Humphrey went back home to Connecticut, returned to Mary and started a family. Now at age eighty-five, he still lives in Connecticut—father, grandfather, businessman, veteran, community leader.

In the years after the war, Sam Humphrey had no way of knowing that back in Louisiana, at the end of 1945, a second message had arrived at Riverside Drive:

The War Department regrets to inform you . . .

Still, Humphrey didn't forgot his sojourn in the Deep South. He and his wife never forgot their weeks as a pair of newlyweds in a Southern family's home. As the years went on, Humphrey joined the Selman Field Historical Association, and began attending veterans' reunions in Monroe. He searched for the name McReynolds every year he came to Louisiana, but Mr. McReynolds had died in 1951 and Mrs. McReynolds in 1967—the family name had disappeared from the town.

Then, in 1995, the Humphreys took a long vacation in the Pacific, a tour of World War II historical sites where, fifty years earlier, as a navigator, Lieutenant Humphrey had flown his combat missions. Their old friend back in Louisiana, Samuel McReynolds, had never mentioned the Philippines when speaking of his son. He had only said: "I have a son missing in the Pacific." One day the Humphreys took a bus tour of Corregidor's battlefield park, and that was the day the name appeared, just outside their bus window: *Capt. Samuel McReynolds.* How could it be anyone else?

They attended the next year's reunion in Monroe with renewed energy. A new piece of the puzzle had been revealed. They visited the church offices of the First Methodist Church, searched through church records. One or two more years went by, however, without any luck. Eventually, they made their way to Monroe's local newspaper, the *News-Star.* There, a long-time *News-Star* editor listened to the Humphreys and, knowing a good story when he heard one, published a small article in his weekly column—an article about Corregidor, about the Humphreys' wartime stay in Monroe, and their search for information on the McReynolds family.

The story might have ended there—except that another resident of Monroe, a woman who recognized the names in the article, made a phone call to a man living in town who, she believed, might be one of the descendants of old Samuel McReynolds.

I am the man she phoned. Samuel McReynolds was my grandfather; Captain McReynolds was my uncle.

I hadn't read the paper that day, and if this complete stranger hadn't phoned me, I might never have learned the story of the Humphreys' search for my family. Naturally, after thanking her, I went straight out and found a copy of the article. All my life, I had known about my West Point uncle who had served at Corregidor, who had never returned from the war. But the connection between my grandparents and the Humphreys was something completely new—new to me, to my brothers and to our cousins.

That same day, I phoned the newspaper offices and spoke with the writer of the article. He was delighted to learn who I was, and he gave me Sam Humphrey's address and telephone number in Connecticut.

The next spring, during the annual Selman Field veterans' reunion, I met Sam Humphrey and his wife Mary. This was the first chance in over fifty years that the Humphreys were able to offer their thanks to a member of the McReynolds family. A word of thanks from two young newlyweds all those years ago; Northern strangers who had been welcomed into a Southern family's home. And I was able to offer the Humphreys my own thanks—for giving my brothers and me a vision of our grandparents that we had never known.

I saw Mr. Humphrey again recently, in the spring of 2008, in Monroe for the annual Selman Field reunion. His wife Mary had died since our last meeting, and he had flown down from Connecticut alone. Mr. Humphrey was eighty-five-years-old, a little slower-moving than years before, but as eager as ever to greet me and to introduce me to his colleagues and fellow-veterans. We spent the afternoon together, speaking of our two families, of the Second World War, of the Pacific campaign, and of two American servicemen who were sent overseas, only one of whom returned. Mr. Humphrey plans to keep coming to Monroe every year as long as he is able.

Solesmes

In the spring of 1974, I was making plans for a backpacking tour of France—my head filled with names such as Icelandic Airlines, Eurail pass, and Kelty outfitters. A few days before departure, an acquaintance suggested that I ought to try to hear some Gregorian chant while I was there. A strange suggestion, I thought.

At the time, I didn't know the first thing about Gregorian chant—nor, at the blithely self-assured age of twenty-four, did I have any interest in Christian liturgy, Catholicism, or any other religious goings-on.

In the year preceding this, I had made friends with a dozen or so young French men and women in Louisiana. They were in the first class of CODOFIL teachers (Council for the Development of French in Louisiana)—an exuberant crowd of French youth, along with some Canadians and Belgians, who arrived here in 1972 and then were scattered more or less willy-nilly about the state. They were assigned to grade schools, middle schools, and high schools to teach French to blasé, softly dozing American students.

With my friends' addresses in hand, I flew to Paris, then took a train to Vendée in the west of France, where one of my hosts lived. I had a vague idea of heading north toward Brittany, briefly east into Belgium, Holland, and Germany, then back into France, all the while stopping at friends' houses along the way—in the best tradition of youthful freeloading.

Now it was June 1974. Pres. Richard Nixon had a couple months left in office. Newspaper heiress Patricia Hearst was still with her captors. The Vietnam War dragged on.

For some reason, before I left Vendée, I asked where one would go to hear Gregorian chant, and my friend's father said that a place in the Loire Valley was just the ticket. It was a Benedictine monastery called the Abbey of Solesmes—a hundred or so miles away, near the town of Le Mans, of racing fame.

The Benedictine order is one of the oldest religious orders of monks, he told me—brothers and priests who live in enclosed communities. He went on with some history about St. Benedict, the sixth century, the Rule of St. Benedict—lessons wasted on me.

Nevertheless, two or three days later I arrived at Sablé-sur-Sarthe, which, as far as I could tell, was the closest train depot to Solesmes.

This was in the days before Internet travel—pre-MapQuest, pre-Travelocity, pre-global-positioning systems, pre-cellphones. You located a spot on a map, got there one way or another, and began asking questions.

Yes, the abbey was two miles away. No, there were no buses or trains. Is there a town nearby called Solesmes? Well, yes, but it's mostly just the abbey and a hotel for Catholic tour buses making the rounds of French religious sites.

Okey-doke. Not having anything better in mind, I started walking. I was on a pleasant, gentle country road, like something out of a Truffaut movie, with lines of swaying trees, an easy breeze, a narrow little river I walked beside, and no hills to speak of. My rucksack was intentionally light.

Eventually I arrived at the edge of a small village—it was about 5 or 5:30 in the afternoon and I could hear bells ringing somewhere ahead.

In my high-school French, I asked a face in a window where the abbey was, and I was pointed farther ahead, up the single main road. The face shouted after me, "Hurry up, you can make vespers, if you run."

It appeared that I was in a typical, small rural French village—at the center of which was a walled collection of stone buildings. One of the buildings was clearly a church. Soon I found a main entrance, a sort of gatehouse with some signs and tourist information.

Inside, I spoke to my first monk—nondescript, amiable, middle-aged. Yes, of course, just throw your backpack under this table and hurry, hurry, you can go out that way, there, yes, toward that door.

Pushing open the massive door to the church was like entering a movie set. Inside, I found a seat in the dim light and waited, not knowing anything. There were no other visitors.

The sound began quietly—literally from far away. From somewhere on my left, the sound grew in volume as it approached, then a door opened and the monks arrived, walking in pairs in a long, slow line, singing as they walked.

They wore black robes—no special dress or vestments—this was a simple vespers service. They filed their way past me and settled into their own places up front—in two halves, facing each other. The singing was in Latin—unaccompanied.

The old cliché was true: I had never heard anything like it in my life. Maybe clichés are about all one has at such moments. I carefully watched the faces of the men as they trooped past at the end of the service. They could have been a collection of Rotarians at any mid-size city in America—young, old, ordinary, grizzled, unremarkable.

It was not until a year later that I read up on the abbey. Without knowing it, I had visited one of the world centers of Gregorian study—renowned to musicians, historians, believers, unbelievers, any and all. Not only was I hearing this sublimely beautiful music for the first time, I was hearing it sung by its premier practitioners.

The distinctive sound of the Solesmes monks is the result of hundreds of years of daily practice, and goes hand in hand with their study of manuscripts, musicology, and liturgy.

It was as if I had stumbled into Oxford University, not aware that it had a fine reputation for scholarship and study. Or as if I had wandered into a performance of the Berlin Philharmonic Orchestra without a clue about what I was hearing.

O days of backpacking! Of ignorance and youth. I was an innocent abroad.

A Year in Ouachita Parish

"Billy, this jalopy is a kidney killer," Bill D. tells me. And he is right. We are driving in his 1951 Willys Jeep down a rutted dirt road called Moccasin Slide. We're steadily swallowing gnats and bugs because the windshield is folded down onto the hood. If it had been up, we wouldn't be able to see—it is so dust-coated. The entire Jeep is covered in dirt and grime—somewhere underneath, it is khaki-colored or dun brown or something—no one is sure anymore. The Jeep resides in a small open-air garage, located down a pathway across from the chicken coop and the workshop, on a branch line of the main driveway. The Jeep-house is hidden from Bill's wife's eyes by more shrubs and trees. There's a twelve-foot johnboat lying nearby, upside-down. A canoe. A boat trailer. Two 35-hp Evinrudes, bolted to wooden stands. Hanging from nails and hooks under the roof of the Jeep-house are fishing poles and rod-and-reels, life preservers, nets, creels, cricket baskets, worm pails.

Moccasin Slide is a mile away. We get to it by driving down a long gravel driveway, briefly onto the state highway (which is not much smoother than a dirt road: "Miss one pothole; hit two"), then a quick jag past a neighbor's house and into the woods. It is late April and the pine trees are thick on both sides of us. If you take a second look into the hills, you can see wild dogwoods blooming, hundreds of them, scattered among the pines, white petals against green needles. They seem to float there, like ghosts, hovering amid the pines. In a few weeks when the petals have fallen, the dogwoods will disappear in a green unbounded fastness.

Bill, a retired surveyor, was born in 1909 in northern Louisiana, in a paper-mill town on the Ouachita River, which, at the time, was a near perfect Snopsian enclave, an unassailable outpost of backwater provincialism. In spite of that, Bill saw Babe Ruth in a traveling exhibition game one year (the Babe went 0 for 5), finished high school, went to work on a road crew, landed in Normandy on D-Day-plus-four, saw combat, saw Paris, advanced into Germany, stepped on a landmine and lost a fist-sized chunk of leg muscle, got shipped stateside, and endured months of rehab in a post-war military hospital. When he finally returned to Louisiana, he found a job with the highway department, married, bought a dozen acres of woodland north of town, and lived there the rest of his life with his wife, year by year transforming their little hillside into a quiet cantonment of vegetable gardens, pastures, workshops, beehives, and out-buildings.

When I knew Bill in the early 1970s, I was a college drop-out, living with my great-aunt on a small farm next to Bill's acreage. Both properties were bounded by a winding two-lane state highway, which made nearly a full circle around us, in its slow, meandering transit from town into the countryside. Within the circle, the ground rose gently to our two neighboring house sites. In Bill's case, the encircled hill was so heavily covered in woods that you couldn't see his house from the road—you couldn't see it from my great-aunt's house either. Pine trees grew at the top of the hill near the houses; hardwoods on the slopes and bottoms. From my great-aunt's house, I had to cross an old garden spot and then follow a deer trail through a patch of broom sage and scrub trees in order to walk to Bill's house. I went there every day.

My walking approach brought me onto his property from the rear, and the first thing I saw was a set of beehives. If I was calm enough, the bees wouldn't bother me—they only became fractious once or twice a year. The hives stood at the edge of Bill's second garden (his "little" garden—used for field peas and a few snap beans—"Better to plant a little extra, Billy," he'd tell me, "for the deer and rabbits to take their share. Because they're going to anyway.") Next to the beehives was a chicken coop—home to eight or ten layers.

Like all of Bill's out-buildings, the chicken coop was made of cypress, occasionally painted, roofed in galvanized steel, sturdy, utilitarian, unlovely, lovely. Shaded by trees and bordered by a pair of bushes—a sweet olive and a camellia.

Bill's hillside was a compound of small cypress buildings. A simple low-slung house held first position at the top of the hill. To get from place to place, you zigzagged down grassy paths, amid shade trees, pine trees, dogwoods, redbuds, and birdhouse poles that had been taken over by Confederate jasmine or yellow jasmine.

Ostensibly, whenever I visited Bill, it was in order to ask his advice about a balky lawnmower, or to borrow a tool ("Careful with that Skilsaw, William; it cuts meat like it cuts wood"), or to set up a meeting with him later that night to watch a baseball game.

Actually, Bill was my only friend those years, 1972 and '73—as well as mentor, guide, woodsman, fisherman, teacher of lore—this sixty-three-year-old countryman, five foot five or six, bald, flat-stomached, fit enough to haul his johnboat onto the top of an ancient Ford station wagon (his fishing car).

Our journey to Moccasin Slide concerns mayhaws. Bill claims to know the whereabouts of a stand of mayhaw trees in a gnarly thicket near Moccasin Creek. We stop the Jeep and find thousands of small red berries on the ground in a boggy stand of exceedingly ugly, spindly-looking, half-stunted trees. I'm scared of snakes in this arboreal ghetto, and Bill tells me to quit being a baby and come along. "I'm not afraid of'em," he says, "if I can see'em." We gather four or five gallons of mayhaws, mostly from the ground, some picked from low branches. Some we assist in falling by running the Jeep's bumper up to the trunk and giving a slight tap. Back at home, Bill's wife commends us, takes the buckets we offer her, shoos us out of the kitchen, so that she can begin her jelly-making.

Our day accomplished, we walk down to the Little House for beers and a dart game. The Little House stands fifty yards below Bill's residence, midway between the workshop and Jeep garage. Except for the barn, it is the principal out-building in the entire compound. Surrounded by its own canopy of shade trees, fronted by a miniature lawn, the Little House is part defunct-camper, part screen porch, about the size of backyard greenhouse (for which it serves every January and February for Bill's wife's plants). Cobbled together over the years, it contains a sink, an electric cook plate, refrigerator, tables, chairs, and the complete paraphernalia for a fish fry—gas cooker, pots, frying baskets, corn meal, gallons of oil. Its existence signifies a certain north Louisiana rural genius, or at least a shrewd bit of marital compromise—removing from kitchen and home, in one stroke, the black plumes of fish-fry smoke, ashtrays, beer cans, the spilled drinks and wreckage of a party or picnic or crawfish boil. The Little House is down the hill and out of sight. It can even be cleaned up—when the need arises—for a proper family gathering or a ladies' Sunday social. There's room in its tiny circular lawn for a hammock, a dozen lawn chairs, a portable record player. People have *lived* in the Little House, in-laws, visiting from St. Louis or Atlanta, who park their motor home behind the building and hook up to the Little House's utilities as if to a campsite. A small purloined Canadian flag hangs from the ceiling inside—the remnant of a crawfish boil Bill and I sponsored in 1975 for a crowd of French and Canadian teachers.

I was twenty-two-years-old in 1972, a refugee from the college days of the 1960s. Once a week in the spare room at my great-aunt's, I awakened from a nightmare, my chest pounding, the sheets sweat-drenched—telling myself, "O.K., O.K., today, you've *got* to see a psychiatrist." I had spent the previous year at LSU (like thousands of others—dutifully enacting the clichés of the era) smoking marijuana, living alone in a dingy apartment, ingesting the occasional capsule of Lord-knows-what. My mother had died the year before (my father died when I was a year-old). My older brothers were all adults, in business, living real lives. We'd sold the house I'd grown up in. When I came tumbling out of LSU, my great-aunt took me in like a storm survivor washed up on the beach.

Years later, in 1984 or 1985, Bill would tell me that he knew how sick I was during that year with my great-aunt. "Your face, your eyes, everything was washed out. It didn't take a doctor to know something was wrong. You looked like some tall, skinny half-grown boy who'd just had the ever-livin' crap knocked out of him. There wasn't anything to do about it, I figured, except wait and watch and see how things turned out. Which is what we did, your great-aunt and me."

All of this was news to me. I hadn't known that I was so transparent at the time. My insides so easily readable by a north Louisiana countryman.

On ordinary days, I would find him outside his storage house/workshop, cleaning a string of bream on a dripping wooden table. Or else repairing a carburetor or an air conditioner or a chainsaw. Bent over his work, intent, talking to a stubborn bolt which will not seat itself, will not make a purchase, "Don't say you're *not going*. Say you don't *want* to go." Then, hearing my approach, looking up, smiling, putting down his cigarette, wiping his hands on his jeans.

I have a lawnmower blade with me that needs sharpening. His grinder is just inside the workshop—a cartoon workshop, containing anything and everything, most of which is on the floor. Hand tools, electric tools, nails, screws, bolts and nuts and washers, a metal storage bin with rusted metal drawers that haven't been opened for five or ten years. Also a coffee can of rusty water for dipping the lawnmower blade into every minute or two to cool it, and an ingenious-looking cone-shaped level, that the blade can be checked for balance with.

Except for the fact that it is truly and actually used every day, the workshop is nearly an *idea* of an American male's garage/shop/storage room, circa 1900-1980. Four or five generations of uncles, fathers, and grandfathers have accumulated these same tools and hardware items, and strewn them in patterns similar to this—in Bill's case, the place looks as if a vagrant wind had entered and given everything a great jumble, sending shelf contents onto floors and floor items onto shelves.

Bill's wife never comes down the hill to the workshop. She doesn't even like to think about the workshop. Indeed it is hidden, isolated (like all the out-buildings) by a ring of fig trees and vines and hedges—saved from being an eyesore by Bill's heterodox landscaping scheme, an accidental design, having to do with the preexistence of certain shade trees and access to water hoses and the length of electric cable Bill happened to have on hand the day he built a particular edifice.

A piece of lawnmower-blade steel shaving has imbedded itself in my thumb, and I ask Bill if he has a pocket knife I can use to extract it. "What do you mean, 'Do I have a pocketknife?'" he says. "Am I wearing pants?"

"Here, give me that thumb," he says. Then flicks the metal out of my hand with a quick stab—one that sends a white-hot searing pain across my brain—but which is over in a millisecond, and sure enough, the offending splinter is gone.

At my great-aunt's house, the nightmares continued through the spring and summer of 1972. I didn't manage to see a doctor. There was no Paxil or Zoloft in 1972, no community centers with free screenings for depression and anxiety. No helpful articles in the newspaper; no armchair psychologists on the Today Show.

Some nights I awakened for another reason. I had fallen in love with a girl I'd known at LSU. She was in Europe that year and I had started writing long letters to her, telling her of my unexpected new life in the outlands of Ouachita Parish. I was hoping through my letters to convince her to love me in return; and sometimes I awakened from a dream where she came to me, embraced me, said, "Yes, you are the one. I love you!" I would sit up in bed with a great jolt of happiness, unable to believe my good luck, then remember where I was, alone in a spare room in my great-aunt's house, in the dreary backwoods of Louisiana.

Sometimes when I walk over to Bill's, no one is home. He and his wife have other lives, after all, besides nursemaiding a mixed-up twenty-two-year-old. Maybe they have driven to town to visit his wife's daughter from a previous marriage (Bill and his wife had no children themselves). Maybe they have gone to the grocery store.

As a matter of fact, I have my own chores waiting on me at my great-aunt's farm. Mowing the yard; mending a stretch of broken fence; feeding cows. I realize that my great-aunt is going to lose patience one day. She hasn't signed on to adopt me. And, indeed, by the end of 1973, I will begin to emerge from my long sabbatical. I will find a job, take up with new friends in town (no drugs, however—those days were over). My hoped-for girl friend returns from Europe, but my love goes unrequited. Heartbreak kills me, doesn't kill me; I fall in love again. And again.

The year 1972 is a year of dispensation, I slowly begin to realize. A gift. My great-aunt and I drive in her Dodge to the grocery story in town, then she drops me off at a tiny branch library for an hour or two. I bring home Faulkner and Borges and English translations of Chinese poetry, and later I read the poems, lying in a hammock between two pine trees. There are tasks to be done on the farm, dogs to be fed, a daily walk down the driveway to the mail box.

In October, Bill and I watch the World Series in Bill's living room. Oakland versus the Cincinnati Reds. The Reds are our favorite team—Johnny Bench, Pete Rose, Joe Morgan with his chicken-wing batting stance. Bill's wife leaves us to our beer and our sports talk. Tippy, a half-Chihuahua, crawls into Bill's lap. His cat, Gray Lady, ambles across the porch. If it's a night game, Bill walks me to the edge of his property at the end of the game—he knows every step in the pitch black night. Past the Little House, past the workshop, chicken house, beehives. At the deer trail, he points me on my way—it's only a hundred yards or so and my great-aunt's dogs will soon scent me and lead me the rest of the way home.

We go fishing in Union Parish north of here. On obscure river-lakes, creeks, bayous, inlets—places known only to surveyors and highway department employees and ancient woodsmen. Saturdays, we visit the livestock auction, sit in the steeply raked seats above the arena (admission is free), and make shrewd comments on the cows and horses parading before us.

One day, we go to a movie, a documentary on Alaska. At the end of summer, you no longer wear a straw cowboy hat when you go to town, but a felt one. We drive to the movie in Bill's new Chevrolet station wagon (the battered old Ford is reserved for fishing), driving down the curving state highway past Mrs. Sandford's grocery and Williams grocery, and the auction barn, and the slaughterhouse, where we once bought a strange blood bait for fishing, past the highway-department offices, past Bill's stepson's construction company, past the house where we take lawnmowers whose ailments are too complicated for us to repair—a house owned by two brothers, one confined to a wheelchair, the other mentally handicapped, but strong as a bull, who together make a single excellent mechanic—past old Solomon's house, a black man who does odd jobs for my great-aunt, past Richard Kimson's house, another black man, who arrives at Bill's house every spring with a mule and plow and turns over the garden spot—not because Bill couldn't do it with his own tiller but because he likes to see the mule work, likes to hear Richard call out gee and haw.

At a farm halfway to town, Bill points toward an overgrown field on my left, "I wish I was bush-hogging that pasture right now."

At a traffic light in town, a shiny car next to us, Bill speaks under his breath, smiling, "Lady, I wish I had that Cadillac and you had a cocklebur up your butt."

After the movie, we talk of war films. "That one called *The Longest Day*," he says. "I could of laughed. It had troops marching in formation down the roads. God almighty, we *never* did that. We'd mostly creep, from tree to tree, on all fours sometimes, scared to death. There was no formation marching, Billy.

"I hope you never go to war. Never. I saw things . . . The French? They were nothing to us. I'd tell them, 'Get the hell out of my way.' There's no words for what I saw.

"This is a picture of me—in my uniform. See Billy, see. I was young once too. I was all right to look at back then. With the women. See? Not bad.

"At Normandy, we were waiting around one day, doing nothing, just waiting. And this company of Rangers came by. They were the sharpest outfit I'd ever seen. Killers, every one of them—trained, steely-eyed killers. Toughest bastards in the army. God, we were impressed by them. They were men!

"Well, I'm sorry. I know you don't want to hear about stuff like that. You're too tender-hearted. But that was how we thought back then. That's who I was."

In November, we made plans to go squirrel hunting one morning. I was to meet him at his carport at daybreak. That night I phoned him, backed out at the last minute.

"It's all right, Billy. It doesn't bother me. I knew you didn't really want to go."

I get a haircut one day. Lop off the last strands of my college long hair, and afterwards I go straight to Bill to let him see what I've done, to receive his approval.

"It looks better, Billy, yes, I admit it, but goddamnit, it doesn't mean that much to me. *You're my friend!* I don't care about stuff like that."

The ice storm hit on the last day of the year. In bed in my great-aunt's house, I awaken to the sound of lumberjacks. Hundreds of lumberjacks, cutting down trees all around us.

The electricity is off. Luckily we have gas heat and a fireplace, which my great-aunt is lighting as I get dressed. When I go outside, I realize that there are no lumberjacks in the area, only thousands of pine limbs cracking at their trunks and falling to the ground. It is a battle zone outdoors. Some of the smaller pines have bent themselves to the ground under the weight—they will stay bent that way for years. The green needles of the pines have collected massive amounts of ice, and the limbs fall all day on our hillside.

I find Bill near the fence that separates our two properties. He has his hammer, staples, and fencing tools. We walk to the highway and make fence repairs where necessary. Absolute silence except for the crack and thud of falling limbs—sometimes they fall behind us, where we just walked.

We check on two neighbors, then return to Bill's house for an enormous breakfast (gas stove). I'm sent home with food for my great-aunt. No cows or horses are loose; no one is harmed. Our hillside will be stranded from the world, without electricity or television or communication for four days, but between my great-aunt and Bill, there are provisions to sustain us for weeks.

I left the hillside in Ouachita Parish a year after the ice storm. Moved to town, found a job, embarked on a young man's new adventures, new disasters. My great-aunt lived to be nearly a hundred. Bill's wife too. Bill died in 1987, at age seventy-eight. Those young pines bent to the ground by the ice storm never straightened and eventually were harvested for pulp wood. For years, between 1972 and 1987, I brought girlfriends and acquaintances out to the country to Bill's house to meet Bill and his wife and drink beer in the Little House. He and I would always part with a bear hug, looking straight into each other's eyes, saying, "I love you, Billy . . . I love you, Bill." He was a retired surveyor, a World War II veteran, a sawed-off untutored childless redneck countryman living in a dismal backwater of northern Louisiana, and, in a year when I absolutely needed him to be so, he was my father.

Sources

Most of the chapters of this book are essays and magazine articles not scholarly works—and thus are not footnoted. The texts cited in the literary essays—novels and short stories—are readily available in libraries. Still, in writing a few of the chapters, I consulted histories, magazine articles, websites, etc. In particular, I read David Lawson's biography, *Paul Morphy: The Pride and Sorrow of Chess*; Seth Cagin and Philip Dray's history of the 1964 civil rights murders, *We Are Not Afraid*; Gerald Clarke's biography, *Capote*; and Mark Kriegel's biography, *Pistol: The Life of Pete Maravich.* And I would never have run across the strange details of the improbable Duke of Brunswick without Prof. Jeremy P. Spinrad's web article on chesscafe.com. Along with these, I am indebted to many other authors for their original research, and, with grateful acknowledgment, I list here a selection of sources for this book:

Andrews, William L., Frances Smith Foster, and Trudier Harris, eds. *The Concise Oxford Companion to African American Literature.* New York: Oxford University Press, 1997.

Ball, Howard. *Murder in Mississippi: United States v. Price and the Struggle for Civil Rights.* Lawrence: University Press of Kansas, 2004.

Barrow, Blanche Caldwell. *My Life with Bonnie & Clyde.* Edited by John Neal Phillips. Norman: University of Oklahoma Press, 2004.

Bradley, A.C. *Shakespearean Tragedy: Lectures on Hamlet, Othello, King Lear, MacBeth.* London: Macmillan, 1950.

Branch, Taylor. *Pillar of Fire: America in the King Years, 1963-65.* New York: Simon & Schuster, 1998.

Brock, Eric J. *New Orleans Cemeteries.* Charleston: Arcadia, 1999.

Cagin, Seth and Philip Dray. *We Are Not Afraid: The Story of Goodman, Schwerner, and Chaney and the Civil Rights campaign for Mississippi.* New York: Macmillan, 1988.

Carter, Hodding, ed. *The Past as Prelude: New Orleans, 1718-1968.* New Orleans: Pelican Publishing House, 1968.

Chardkoff, Richard B. *World War II Aerial Navigation Training & The Flyboy Heroes of Selman Field.* Lafayette, LA: Center for Louisiana Studies, 2008.

Clarke, Gerald. *Capote: A Biography.* New York: Simon & Schuster, 1988.

Comolli, Jean-Louis and André S. Labarthe. "Conversation with Arthur Penn." *Cahiers du Cinéma*, no. 196 (1967).

Currie, Stephen. *Murder in Mississippi: The 1964 Freedom Summer Killings.* San Diego: Lucent Books, 2006.

Edge, Frederick Milne. *The Exploits and Triumphs in Europe of Paul Morphy.* New York: Pelican Publishing Company, 1973.

Fossier, Albert E. *New Orleans: The Glamour Period, 1800-1840.* New Orleans: American Printing Company, Ltd., 1957.

Friedman, Lester D. *Arthur Penn's Bonnie and Clyde.* Cambridge: Cambridge University Press, 2000.

———. *Bonnie and Clyde.* London: British Film Industry Publishing, 2000.

Heffron, Jack and Mark Garvey. "Fake Bullets in Louisiana," *The Oxford American Magazine*, no. 29 (September/October, 1999).

Hendrickson, Paul. *Sons of Mississippi: A Story of Race and its Legacy.* New York: Knopf, 2003.

Hinton, Ted, as told to Larry Grove. *Ambush: The Real Story of Bonnie and Clyde.* Austin, TX: Shoal Creek Publishers, 1979.

Keyes, Frances Parkinson. *The Chess Players.* New York: Farrar, Straus and Cudahy, 1960.

Kriegel, Mark. *Pistol: The Life of Pete Maravich.* New York: Free Press, 2007.

Lawson, David. *Paul Morphy: The Pride and Sorrow of Chess.* New York: David McKay Company, Inc., 1976.

"The Life and Chess of Paul Morphy." http://batgirl.atspace.com/index.html.

Marrs, Suzanne. *Eudora Welty: A Biography.* Orlando: Harcourt, 2005.

McAdam, Doug. *Freedom Summer.* New York: Oxford University Press, 1988.

McAlexander, Hubert Horton. *Peter Taylor: A Writer's Life.* Baton Rouge: Louisiana State University Press, 2001.

Menand, Louis. "Paris, Texas," *New Yorker* 79, no. 1 (February 17, 2003): 169.

Milner, E.R. *The Lifes and Times of Bonnie and Clyde.* Carbondale: Southern Illinois University Press, 1996.

Moates, Marianne M. *A Bridge of Childhood: Truman Capote's Southern Years.* New York: Henry Holt and Company, 1995.

Percy, Walker. *Lancelot.* New York: Farrar, Straus and Giroux, 1977.

Phillips, John Neal. *Running with Bonnie and Clyde: The Ten Fast Years of Ralph Fults.* Norman: University of Oklahoma Press, 1996.

Prenshaw, Peggy Whitman, ed. *Conversations with Eudora Welty.* Jackson: University Press of Mississippi, 1984.

Schlueter, Paul. *Shirley Ann Grau.* Boston: Twayne Publishing, 1981.

Schultz, Debra L. *Going South: Jewish Women in the Civil Rights Movement*. New York: New York University Press, 2001.

Selman Field: World War II: 1942-1946. Paducah, KY: Turner Publishing Company, 1998.

Spinrad, Jeremy P. "New Stories about Old Chess Players." http://chesscafe.com/archives/archives.htm.

Steele, Phillip W. *The Family Story of Bonnie and Clyde*. Gretna, LA: Pelican Publishing Company, 2000.

Tolson, Jay. *Pilgrim in the Ruins: A Life of Walker Percy*. New York: Simon & Schuster, 1992.

Treherne, John. *The Strange History of Bonnie and Clyde*. New York: Cooper Square Press, 2000.

Waldron, Ann. *Eudora: A Writer's Life*. New York: Doubleday, 1998.

Ward, Chris, *The Genius of Paul Morphy*. London: Cadogan Chess, 1997.

Internet sources make the traditional researcher uneasy, yet it's hard to imagine a magazine writer who does not Google a subject under investigation or who does not consult Wikipedia. Without the internet, I doubt that I'd have discovered the British-made 35mm film projector, the Gaumont-Kalee, or the classic, weapons-grade office-stapler, the Swingline #4. Along with two sites listed above, here are some selections from the websites I consulted:

http://cinematreasures.org/

http://dictionary.reference.com/

http://en.wikipedia.org/wiki/Main_Page

http://frankoconnor.ucc.ie/dateline.php

http://kilcullenbridge.blogspot.com/2006/07/projecting-images-of-life.html

http://www.arnabontempsmuseum.com/

http://www.geocities.com/typewriterexchange/Swingline.html

http://www.historictheatres.org/

http://www.lib.utk.edu/refs/tnauthors/authors/bontemps-a.html

http://www.officemuseum.com/staplers.htm

http://www.regalgroup.org.uk/collectiongallery.html

http://www.scottishcinemas.org.uk/edinburgh/proj_memories.html

Credits

Essays not listed are published for the first time in this collection.

"Bullets and Bodies." *The Oxford American*, no. 56, Movie Issue (2007).

"The Unenthusiastic Chess Champion of the World." *The Oxford American*, no. 59, Sports Issue (2007).

"Ode to a Hoop Star." *The Oxford American*, no. 61, Best of the South Issue (2008).

"The Movie Theater: A Dream" as "Cinema Paradiso." *The Oxford American*, no. 60, Home Issue (2008).

"The Best Southern Short Story Ever?" *The Oxford American*, no. 53 (2006). [Reprinted in *The Writer's Presence*, Sixth Edition. New York: Bedford/St. Martin's, 2009.]

"Amid the Swirling Ghosts." *The Oxford American*, no. 52 (2006). [Reprinted in SIRS Renaissance Database; www.proquest.com.]

"Portrait of the Spinster As a Young Woman." *The Oxford American*, no. 57, Best of the South Issue (2007).

"Best Southern Short Story with a Drowned Bride, Alligators, a Fish Fry, some light S&M, French Cinema, the Pearl River, Mel Gibson, and a Chicken" as "A River Runs Through It." *The Oxford American*, no. 65, Best of the South Issue (2009).

"How Far Into Grief, Disaster, or Horror?" *The Oxford American*, no. 55 (2006).

"Quartered." *The Oxford American*, no. 62, New Orleans/Gulf Coast Issue (2008).

"The Piano Player." *The Oxford American*, no. 63, Music Issue (2008).

"A Day on the Town" as "A Joy-filled Day on the Town." *The Christian Science Monitor*, February 28, 2008.

"A Concise History of Country Music." *The Oxford American*, no. 54, Music Issue (2006).

"French Baseball" as "What is this game, le baseball?" *The Christian Science Monitor*, August 15, 2008.

"Fastened" as "The Louisiana Workman's Trusty Tool." *The Christian Science Monitor*, December 2, 2008.

"Solesmes" as "The Wonder of Gregorian Chant." *The Christian Science Monitor*, October 25, 2007.